GAY

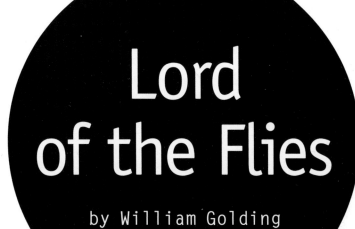

Lord
of the Flies

by William Golding

Robert Francis

Series Editors:

Sue Bennett and Dave Stockwin

HODDER
EDUCATION
AN HACHETTE UK COMPANY

The Publishers would like to thank the following for permission to reproduce copyright material.

Photo credits

pp. 9, 11, 14 TopFoto; **p.18** PPP3/Fotolia; **pp. 20,45** Photos12/Alamy; **pp.31,33,35,40** Orion Pictures/Pictorial Press.com; **p. 54** Pictorial Press/Alamy.

Acknowledgements

p.10 William Golding Ltd. Extracts from *Lord of the Flies* reproduced by permission of Faber and Faber Ltd (applied for), and G.P. Putnam's Sons, an imprint of Penguin Publishing Group, a division of Penguin Random House LLC.

Every effort has been made to trace all copyright holders, but if any have been inadvertently overlooked, the Publishers will be pleased to make the necessary arrangements at the first opportunity.

Although every effort has been made to ensure that website addresses are correct at time of going to press, Hodder Education cannot be held responsible for the content of any website mentioned in this book. It is sometimes possible to find a relocated web page by typing in the address of the home page for a website in the URL window of your browser.

Hachette UK's policy is to use papers that are natural, renewable and recyclable products and made from wood grown in sustainable forests. The logging and manufacturing processes are expected to conform to the environmental regulations of the country of origin.

Orders: please contact Bookpoint Ltd, 130 Park Drive, Milton Park, Abingdon, Oxon OX14 4SE. Telephone: (44) 01235 827720. Fax: (44) 01235 400454. Email education@bookpoint.co.uk Lines are open from 9 a.m. to 5 p.m., Monday to Saturday, with a 24-hour message answering service. You can also order through our website: www.hoddereducation.co.uk

ISBN: 978 1 4718 5361 6

© Robert Francis, 2016

First published in 2016 by

Hodder Education,

An Hachette UK Company

Carmelite House

50 Victoria Embankment

London EC4Y 0DZ

www.hoddereducation.co.uk

Impression number		5	4	3	2	1
Year		2020	2019	2018	2017	2016

Cover photo © Ron Dahlquist/Getty Images/Design Pics RF/Thinkstock

Typeset in 11/13pt Bliss Light by Integra Software Services Pvt. Ltd., Pondicherry, India

Printed in Italy

A catalogue record for this title is available from the British Library.

Contents

Getting the most from this guide 5

1 Introduction 6

2 Context 9

3 Plot and structure 17

4 Characterisation 30

5 Themes 42

6 Language, style and analysis 49

7 Tackling the exams 57

8 Assessment Objectives and skills 67

9 Sample essays 72

10 Top ten 91

Wider reading 98

Answers 99

Getting the most from this guide

This guide is designed to help you to raise your achievement in your examination response to *Lord of the Flies*. It is written so that you can use it throughout your GCSE English Literature course: it will help you when you are studying the novel for the first time and also during your revision.

The following features have been used throughout this guide to help you focus your understanding of the novel:

Target your thinking

A list of **introductory questions** labelled by Assessment Objective is provided at the beginning of each section to give you a breakdown of the material covered. They target your thinking, in order to help you work more efficiently by focusing on the key messages.

Build critical skills

These boxes offer an opportunity to consider some **more challenging questions**. They are designed to encourage deeper thinking, analysis and exploratory thought. Building and practising your critical skills in this way will give you a real advantage in the examination.

GRADE *FOCUS*

It is possible to know a novel well and yet still underachieve in the examination if you are unsure what the examiners are looking for. The **GRADE FOCUS** boxes give a clear explanation of **how you may be assessed**, with an emphasis on the criteria for gaining a Grade 5 and a Grade 8.

REVIEW YOUR LEARNING

At the end of each chapter you will find this section to **test your knowledge**: a series of short, specific questions to ensure you have understood and absorbed the key messages of the section. Answers to the 'Review your learning' questions are provided in the final section of the guide (p. 99).

GRADE *BOOSTER*

Read and remember these pieces of helpful **grade-boosting advice**. They provide top tips from experienced teachers and examiners who can advise you on what to do, as well as what *not* to do, in order to maximise your chances of success in the examination.

Key quotation

Key quotations are highlighted for you, so that if you wish you may use them as **supporting evidence** in your examination answers. Further quotations grouped by characterisation, key moments and theme can be found in the 'Top ten' section on page 91 of the guide. All page references in this guide refer to the 2002 edition of *Lord of the Flies*, published by Faber and Faber (ISBN 978-0-571191-47-5).

'The rules!...You're breaking the rules!'
(p. 99)

Introduction

Studying the text

You may find it useful to read sections of this guide when you need them, rather than reading it from start to finish. For example, the section on 'Context' can be read before you read the novel itself, since it offers an explanation of the relevant historical, cultural and literary background to the text. It is here where you will find information about aspects of Golding's life and times which influenced his writing, the particular issues with which he was concerned and where the novel stands in terms of the literary context to which it belongs.

As you work through the novel, you may find it helpful to read the relevant parts of the 'Plot and structure' section before or after reading a particular chapter. As well as a summary of events there is also commentary, so that you are aware both of key events and features in each of the chapters. Later, the sections on 'Characterisation', 'Themes' and 'Language, style and analysis' will help to develop your thinking further, in preparation for written responses on particular aspects of the text.

Many students enjoy the experience of being able to bring something extra to their classroom lessons in order to be 'a step ahead of the game'. Alternatively, you may have missed a classroom session or feel that you need a clearer explanation, and the guide can help you with this too.

An initial reading of the section on 'Assessment Objectives and skills' will enable you to make really effective notes in preparation for assessments. The Assessment Objectives are what exam boards base their mark schemes on. In this section they are broken down and clearly explained.

Revising the text

Whether you study the novel in a block of time close to the exam or much earlier in your GCSE English Literature course, you will need to revise thoroughly if you are to achieve the very best grade that you can.

You should first remind yourself of what happens in the novel, and so the section on 'Plot and structure' might be the best starting point for revision. You might then look at the 'Assessment Objectives and skills' section to ensure that you understand what the examiners are looking for in general, and then look carefully at 'Tackling the exams'. This section gives you useful information on question format, depending on which exam board specification you are following, as well as practical advice on the examination format, and practical considerations such as the time available for the question and the Assessment Objectives that apply to it.

Advice is also supplied on how to approach the question, writing a quick plan, and 'working with' the text. Focused advice on how you might improve your grade follows, and you need to read this section carefully.

You will also find examples of exam-style responses in the 'Sample essays' section, with examiner comments in the margins, so that you can see clearly how to move towards a Grade 5 and how to then move from Grade 5 to Grade 8.

Now that all GCSE English Literature examinations are 'closed book', the 'Top ten' section will be an invaluable aid, in that it offers you the opportunity to learn short quotations to support points about character and themes as well as a revision aid which identifies the top ten key moments in the novel's development.

When writing about the novel, use this guide as a springboard to develop your own ideas. Remember that the examiners are not looking for set responses, so never try to memorise chunks of this guide to regurgitate in the exam. Identical answers are dull. The examiners hope to reward you for perceptive thought, individual appreciation and varying interpretations. They want to sense that you have engaged with the themes and ideas in the novel and that you have explored Golding's methods with an awareness of the context in which he wrote. Above all, don't be afraid to make it clear that you have enjoyed the novel.

There are two film versions of *Lord of the Flies*: the classic 1963 black-and-white film directed by Peter Brook which is very close to the text and the 1990 Harry Hook version which is adapted from the novel and presents the boys as American, surviving on the island. You will find interesting differences between them; for example, the language has been Americanised in the 1990 version, and the 1963 version is much darker both in lighting and in the way the events are presented. Both versions of the story convey the essential messages of the novel. However, they should never be seen as a substitute for the text itself. For example, examiners are unlikely to be impressed by responses which refer to the actors or the director of the film.

Enjoy referring to the guide as you study the text, and good luck in your exam.

Context

Target your thinking

- What is meant by 'context'? (**AO3**)
- How does Golding relate the events on the island to those in the wider world? (**AO3**)
- What use does he make of the fears of people in the 1950s? (**AO3**)
- How has Golding used his own experiences in the novel? (**AO3**)

What is 'context'?

Knowledge of context will help you to understand and appreciate your reading of *Lord of the Flies*, but what exactly is it?

'Context' is a wide-ranging term. It refers to the historical, socioeconomic and political circumstances of the time, as well as to the author's beliefs about those circumstances. It also refers to the way that more personal events in the author's own life may have influenced his thinking and writing. Finally, it may also refer to literary context and be concerned with developments in the novel as a form which may also have influenced the way it was written.

Lord of the Flies was written in the early 1950s and published in 1954.

GRADE BOOSTER

It is important to have some knowledge of Golding's life as well as the context of the novel.

This will help you to understand the author's purposes and concerns as well as any contemporary issues which may have affected the presentation of characters or themes.

However, there is little to be gained by simply 'bolting on' biographical or cultural details. They must always be related to the question you are answering.

▲ William Golding in later life (1983)

Golding and *Lord of the Flies*

William Golding was born in Cornwall in 1911. Like Jack in *Lord of the Flies*, he is said to have been a bully as a young boy and has described himself as a 'brat', someone who 'enjoyed hurting people'.

Here is an extract from one of his autobiographical works, *Scenes from a life*, in which he discusses how violence can develop even from innocent beginnings:

> I swung the bat in a semicircle, missed the ball but hit José with the wooden bat across the side of the head. Instantly he turned and ran for home, one hand holding the side of his head. I was the one who made a noise, anguished to think of the awful thing I had done. But he made not a sound. He always was the silent one. I trundled after him, whimpering and wondering what I should tell mam and dad, or what he would.
>
> I trundled back across the Common and down the road to the Green, my fears growing deeper. I can just remember them. I ended at the house, terrified and now as silent as my brother. I remember no more. But years later my parents told me that José had described the whole scene to them. He wasn't really hurt they said. But I crept in to the house with my terror and hid from everyone else under the dining room table.

The violence in *Lord of the Flies* starts as a game. The game goes too far and the potential for the extreme savagery that follows can be seen in all the boys except Simon. Even Ralph and Piggy become involved in the dance that leads to the death of Simon.

Golding's father was a rationalist: someone who believes that we can best understand the world through the application of reason. Although he was very influenced by his father as a young boy, and studied at the grammar school where his father taught, he later appeared to see the rationalist approach as having limitations, becoming more interested in deeper, philosophical or mystical matters.

In 1935 Golding became a teacher. His subjects were English and philosophy, the latter interest being reflected in some of the important questions raised in the novel. As a teacher, he learnt at first hand of the savagery and cruelty of which young boys are capable. Later he used this knowledge to inform his writing of *Lord of the Flies*.

During the Second World War, Golding served in the British Navy, on several different ships, and was in charge of specially adapted landing craft for the D-Day landings in Normandy, so he witnessed the horrors of war, including the effects of his own actions as a naval officer. He came to the conclusion that human beings are not naturally kind and that 'man produces evil as a bee produces honey.'

Lord of the Flies was published in 1954, a time when the possibility of a nuclear war was a real threat. The novel reflects in several ways Golding's interest in the existence of evil, including the idea of the beast and the boys' degeneration into savagery against the background of the war. The title of the book is a reference to Beelzebub (a Hebrew word for the Devil), who is the God of the Fly (translated as 'Lord of the Flies'). This is most clearly evident when the pig's head appears to speak to Simon.

The Second World War

Britain declared war on Germany on 3 September 1939, and the war in Europe lasted for almost six years. In the novel, Golding explores some of the ideas that lay behind the Nazi government of Germany.

- The German leader Adolf Hitler adapted ideas from science and philosophy for his own ends. Compare Hitler's ideas of racial purity and the supremacy of the Aryan race with Darwin's theory of natural selection and survival of the fittest (see the 'Themes' section p. 42 for more detail). On the island, the boys have varying degrees of physical and mental strength. You need to think about which characteristics Golding portrays as gaining supremacy.

- One of the most feared of the Nazi organisations was the SS (*Schutzstaffel*: defence corps). The SS was fiercely loyal to Hitler and was renowned for never showing human weakness. The often brutal way in which the SS treated its enemies is similar to the way Jack uses Roger to terrify the other boys into submission.

▲ The Hitler Youth in Nazi Germany

Life in 1950s Britain

Rationing

Food rationing had been a part of people's lives in Britain since the start of the Second World War. Schoolchildren in the early 1950s had grown up without knowing what it was like to have a wide range of food readily available.

The lack of food in Britain throughout the war and even into the early post-war years was a major influence on people's lives. Although people had enough food to survive, meat in any quantity and imported fruit such as oranges and bananas became luxuries. Food plays a major part in *Lord of the Flies* – look at the availability of food on the island. It is the desire to hunt for meat that causes many of the problems between the boys. When they first land on the island, they collect food whenever they are hungry. Later, hunting becomes a major driving force behind Jack's actions, although this is about far deeper urges than just hunger for food.

Key quotation

'He tried to convey the compulsion to track down and kill that was swallowing him up.'
(p. 51)

Hardship

Large areas of British cities had suffered severe damage from German bombing. By the 1950s, rebuilding work was under way but there were still many devastated areas. There was a shortage of many everyday items and 'making do and mending' was still common practice in most homes. Clothes were difficult to obtain and so repairing them was essential. We may see hardships in today's society, but for very different reasons and of a very different kind.

Keeping up appearances was a very British way of dealing with hardship. Look at the importance that clothes play in representing civilised society in the novel. When Ralph, Piggy, Sam and Eric go to Castle Rock at the end of the book they attempt to dress themselves as English schoolboys, as though this will make their requests more acceptable to Jack.

Attitudes

The Second World War cost Britain its empire. At its height, the British Empire was seen as the greatest the world had known. It spread across the whole globe and the saying 'The sun never sets on the British Empire' had been literally true: somewhere in the empire it was daytime no matter what the time was in Britain. In Britain, the upper and middle classes had grown up with the idea that it was natural for them to be in charge and to organise others. This idea is expressed several times in the novel: that simply being English means that certain things are expected. However, perhaps the novel subverts ideas about British moral superiority as it was not uncommon to condemn the Japanese and Germans for cruelty and savagery while believing ourselves to be blameless. It might be argued that the novel is suggesting that these tendencies are in humanity as a whole.

Class

In the 1950s the class system in Britain was still rigid. Knowing your place was still an accepted idea in Britain. It was difficult for people born into poor, working-class backgrounds to rise in society. At the start of the novel, the boys have a clear sense of their own relative importance.

Very broadly speaking, society could be divided into three main strands.

The upper class

The upper class consisted mainly of aristocratic families with inherited money that came mostly from huge estates of land. It is worth reflecting that in the early part of the twentieth century, 1% of the population owned 99% of the wealth. The aristocracy had been in decline since the late 1930s but still held great power. Upper-class boys were educated at prestigious public schools such as Eton, Harrow and Marlborough (see the section on schools on p. 14).

The middle class

This was a much wider group than the upper class. The middle classes made their money through business or the professions. Such people would want their children to have a good start in life, and would often imitate the upper-class practice of sending their children, particularly boys, to public schools – probably 'minor' public schools that did not have the status of Eton or Harrow.

The boys in *Lord of the Flies* are typical examples of middle-class children of the 1950s. There is no evidence that their families are particularly wealthy: Ralph's father is in the Navy and Piggy's aunt does not seem to be wealthy. This perhaps explains why Piggy has such a low status with the other boys, despite the fact that he is more intelligent than most of the others.

The working class

The working class were mainly those who worked in manual trades or unskilled and semi-skilled clerical positions. Many worked in the factories, shops and businesses owned by the middle classes. Working-class education was limited and offered few opportunities for social mobility. Until the Butler Education Act of 1944, many children left school at the age of 14 with only a basic schooling.

Before the Second World War it had been virtually impossible for working-class people to mix on equal terms with their 'betters'. In the 1950s the situation gradually began to change, with new opportunities

Build critical skills

If working-class belief was that they were ruled by their betters (i.e. consensus politics), is the behaviour of the boys (especially as future leaders) another jolt to 1950s complacency?

How important are adults and the world of adults to Piggy and Ralph in Chapter 1? What does this show about the role of adults in their lives and the novel?

Look specifically at the passage in Chapter 1 from:

'I could swim when I was five. Daddy taught me.'

to

'About the atom bomb? They're all dead.' (pp. 8–9)

in the Britain that was emerging from the wreckage of the war. This has continued to develop up to the present day although there are still concerns about social mobility, particularly for the poorest in our society.

▲ Schoolboys in the 1950s

Public schools and grammar schools

The class system and the education system were closely linked. Public schools were, and still are, fee-paying schools. By contrast the 1944 Education Act introduced free grammar schools across the country. These were often single-sex schools and required pupils to pass an exam at the age of 11 – the '11-plus'. Grammar schools kept the uniform and traditions of the public schools and were seen as providing an academic education for bright children who could otherwise not afford it. Children who failed the 11-plus went to secondary modern schools to learn more practical subjects. In practice, many more middle-class than working-class children went to grammar schools, while most working-class children went to the secondary moderns.

The boys in *Lord of the Flies* appear to be typical of the kinds of boys who would go to public schools at age 13 or grammar schools at 11.

When you discuss this aspect of the novel, you should remember that Golding was a qualified teacher who not only attended a grammar school himself but also worked at a boys' grammar school for many years, both before and after the war.

Build critical skills

What do we learn about the education the boys have had before arriving on the island? How does Golding present information about the way the boys have been educated at home? How does this education affect their behaviour now?

The Cold War

Following the Second World War, Britain's former ally, the Soviet Union, became the potential enemy of the West. The major nuclear powers were the USA and the Soviet Union, with the USA's NATO (North Atlantic Treaty Organization) allies such as Britain and France following closely behind. Throughout the 1950s, people in Britain feared the threat of Soviet nuclear attack. The Allied nuclear attacks on Nagasaki and Hiroshima at the end of the Second World War brought home to people what nuclear war meant. The Soviet and NATO forces were separated by the flimsiest of borders, and nuclear weapons situated in Ukraine could have reached the UK in such a short time that few people would have survived even if British missiles had been fired as soon as the attack was detected. The nuclear stand-off became known as Mutually Assured Destruction (MAD), as it would have led to the destruction of both attacker and attacked – no one could win.

The novel is set against the backdrop of a nuclear war. However, it also subtly explores the idea of Mutually Assured Destruction within its own plot. The final fire destroys the world of the island. If the naval officer had not arrived, how would Jack's tribe have survived its 'victory'?

Literary context

Boys' adventure books

Lord of the Flies follows a tradition of adventure books aimed mainly at boys – generally, girls were not encouraged to seek adventure before the 1950s. In Chapter 2 the boys liken their situation to *Treasure Island*, *Swallows and Amazons* and *The Coral Island*. Such books were very popular, particularly with young boys like those in the novel.

The reference to the coral island in Chapter 1 is a link to the novel *The Coral Island* by R. M. Ballantyne. Both novels are about boys shipwrecked on an island. However, the boys in Ballantyne's novel behave impeccably and are models of old-fashioned Britishness. This novel was clearly in Golding's mind when writing *Lord of the Flies*. He wanted to question the idea that boys without adult guidance would behave so perfectly and rationally, and to explore the darker nature of humanity, using the island as a microcosm.

However, the novel may also seen as allegorical. An allegory is a simple story, designed to teach a moral lesson which can be read on more than one level. It is in many ways similar to a fable, which often features one-dimensional talking animals. *Lord of the Flies* is allegorical in that the characters represent different groups of people. For example, Piggy can be seen as representing intellectuals, and the outsider Simon as representing

Key quotation

'We'll have to have "Hands up" like at school.'
(p. 31)

Since the novel was written, society has changed and our view of the novel will be very different from that of readers when it was originally published in 1954. In the twenty-first century, are we still as shocked by the idea of children who kill? What else might we see differently?

mystics or visionaries. Although it can be read on one level as a story of what happens to a group of boys when shipwrecked, it can also be read as a story with a much deeper meaning in its exploration of the evil inside us all and the ways in which evil can flourish in the world.

GRADE FOCUS

Grade 5

To achieve Grade 5, students will show a clear understanding of the context in which the novel was written.

Grade 8

To achieve Grade 8, students will make perceptive, critical comments about the ways that contextual factors affect the choices that the writer makes.

REVIEW YOUR LEARNING

(Answers are given on p. 99.)

1 What is meant by the 'context' of a novel?
2 *Lord of the Flies* is often seen as a more realistic version of which novel?
3 How did Golding's pre- and post-war profession add to his understanding of boys' behaviour?
4 What is an 'allegory'?
5 What period in Golding's life led him to believe that evil was a part of man?
6 How does the boys' schooling affect their behaviour on the island?

Plot and structure

Target your thinking

- What are the main events of the novel? (**AO1**)
- How do the main storylines develop through the novel? (**AO1/AO2**)
- How does Golding use structure? (**AO2**)

Plot

Chapter 1 The sound of the shell

Summary

- Ralph and Piggy call the other boys together.
- Ralph is made leader but Jack keeps the choir.
- Ralph, Jack and Simon learn that they are on an island.

Commentary

The novel opens with Ralph clambering through the jungle towards the lagoon. He is accompanied by Piggy (who has not yet told Ralph his nickname).

From the boys' conversation we learn that they were in a plane that had been attacked and which then crashed on the island. It soon dawns on the boys that there are probably no adults left alive.

The plane crash is a deliberate ploy by Golding: the boys have no means of reconstructing England from the wreckage. They are alone with whatever tools and other aids to survival they can fashion for themselves.

Piggy tells Ralph that he heard the pilot saying that an atom bomb had gone off and no one was left to look for them. He finds a conch shell and, when Ralph blows the conch, boys begin to appear from the jungle. The younger boys wait patiently to be told what to do.

As soon as Jack arrives, leading his choir, he begins to assert himself, and he is the only boy who speaks to Ralph on equal terms.

Ralph lifts the conch and says that there should be a chief to decide things. Jack immediately says that he should be the chief. The boys, however, attracted by Ralph's quiet authority and the fact that he has blown the conch, quickly elect him as chief.

> **Build critical skills**
>
> How does Golding make Jack and the choir seem less human than the other boys? (p. 15) Why does he do this?

> **Build critical skills**
>
> Read the passage from 'The children who came along the beach' to 'eccentric clothing' (pp. 14–15).
>
> How does Golding use **foreshadowing** here?

Ralph, Jack and Simon explore the area and find a piglet trapped in the undergrowth: Jack draws his knife, but hesitates, which allows the animal to escape. This is the reader's first glimpse of Jack's willingness to kill. Though he hesitates here, this incident is a clear indication that he is capable of being savage.

Key quotation

'...he hadn't: because of the enormity of the knife descending and cutting into living flesh; because of the unbearable blood.'
(p. 29)

Chapter 2 Fire on the mountain

Summary

- The small boys begin to worry about a beast.
- A signal fire is lit, with the choir responsible for keeping it going.
- The forest catches fire and at least one boy is killed.

Commentary

Jack interrupts the second meeting to announce that they will need hunters to catch pigs. He gets excited by the idea of inventing rules, especially so that those who break them can be punished.

Ralph decides that the conch will be passed to anyone who asks to speak and that the person with the conch will not be interrupted. The use of the conch is a child's version of order.

One of the smaller boys says that he has seen a giant snake that he calls the 'beastie', which came at night and tried to eat him.

Ralph tells the boys that they need to light a fire on the mountain top to attract the attention of passing ships. Jack realises that Piggy's glasses can be used to light the fire.

Jack begins to change the rules even at this early stage, mostly to suit himself, foreshadowing the way he behaves later in the novel.

Ralph announces that the conch counts no matter where it is used.

Piggy notices that the fire has set the surrounding forest ablaze and at least one of the younger boys might have been caught in the forest fire.

▲ The conch: a symbol of power

Chapter 3 Huts on the beach

Summary

- Jack becomes more interested in hunting.
- Ralph tries to get the boys to build shelters.

Build critical skills

The boys begin to feel an impact, and even a threat, from the natural world that surrounds them. They are unsure how to react. The small boys are scared and even Jack feels he is being hunted. How would you explain their fears at this point? Are they simply 'imagining things', or is there something real to be afraid of?

GRADE BOOSTER

Exploring symbolism can help you achieve a higher grade. For example, the fire is a symbol of the power of the forces of nature. The boys think they can control the situation, but stopping the fire is soon beyond their power.

Commentary

Jack is in the forest on his own, tracking pigs. He has now made himself a spear and still carries a large knife.

Ralph realises that Jack is intent on killing but asks for his help with the shelters. Jack insists that he needs to catch meat for the group. Ralph and Jack both come close to losing their tempers but refuse to compromise their own point of view.

The 'littluns' are becoming frightened at night because they think that there is something in the forest that will come to get them. Jack feels that he is not alone when he is in the forest but that he is being hunted, even though he is supposedly the one hunting.

Key quotation

'We ought to have more rules. Where the conch is, that's a meeting.'
(p. 42)

Key quotation

'"That little 'un—" gasped Piggy – "him with the mark on his face, I don't see him. Where is he now?"'
(p. 46)

Build critical skills

Many of the most important symbols of the novel are introduced in this chapter: the fire, the conch, Piggy's glasses and the beast. How does Golding present these symbols and what impact does this have on the novel at this point?

Chapter 4 Painted faces and long hair

Summary

- Smoke from a ship is seen on the horizon.
- The fire has gone out.
- Jack nearly stands up to Ralph.
- Piggy's glasses are partly broken by Jack.
- The pig is killed.
- The boys have a feast of roast pig.

Commentary

The boys play on the beach and we are introduced to some of the other characters, such as Henry, Percival, Roger and Maurice. Jack is experimenting with camouflaging his face so that the pigs cannot see him so easily. However, as we will gradually see, this face painting is also a means of escaping from the constraints of civilised society.

Key quotation

'the mask was a thing on its own, behind which Jack hid, liberated from shame and self-consciousness.'
(p. 66)

Key quotation

'They walked along, two continents of experience and feeling, unable to communicate.'
(p. 56)

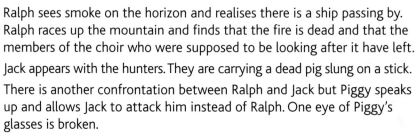

Build critical skills

Read the passage beginning 'Jack was standing under a tree' and ending with 'The mask compelled them' (pp. 65–67).

How does Golding present Jack here and what might he be suggesting by presenting Jack in this way? (Think about connections to ancient societies that also practised this ceremonial behaviour.)

Ralph sees smoke on the horizon and realises there is a ship passing by. Ralph races up the mountain and finds that the fire is dead and that the members of the choir who were supposed to be looking after it have left.

Jack appears with the hunters. They are carrying a dead pig slung on a stick.

There is another confrontation between Ralph and Jack but Piggy speaks up and allows Jack to attack him instead of Ralph. One eye of Piggy's glasses is broken.

Ralph asserts his authority and Jack backs down a little, but it is clear he now has the admiration of many of the boys because he has brought them meat.

The fire is relit and the boys feast on the pig.

Chapter 5 Beast from water

Summary

- Ralph calls an assembly.
- The boys find it hard to listen to sensible ideas.

▲ Jack with a painted face

- The idea of the beast is discussed.
- Jack rebels.

Commentary

Ralph calls an important assembly to discuss the fire and the way the boys live on the island. At first the boys listen to his points, which are:

- No one is collecting fresh water any longer.
- The shelters have not been built properly because most of the boys got bored and gave up.
- The rocks are no longer being used as a lavatory.
- The fire is the most important thing.
- The only fire is to be on the mountain.
- There is no beast.

Many of the younger boys are convinced that there is a beast on the island. One of the small boys, Percival, says that the beast comes from the sea. Even Simon says that there may be a beast, which undermines Ralph in front of the others.

The rule whereby a boy must be holding the conch to speak starts to break down and Jack defies Ralph.

Jack leads the choir away and the assembly dissolves, leaving Ralph looking powerless. Ralph, Piggy and Simon are left wishing there was an adult present to tell them what to do and to reassure them.

The remaining boys long for adult intervention. They make several ironic comments about adults: 'They wouldn't quarrel', 'Or break my specs', 'Or talk about a beast' (p. 102). Yet all these are aspects of many adults. Adults argue, commit acts of violence on each other and have strong superstitious beliefs. Golding is making the point that the boys are a reflection of the adult world beyond the island.

Chapter 6 Beast from air

Summary

- An airman, who is dead, lands on the island, still in his parachute.
- Sam and Eric hear something strange on the mountain.

Commentary

During the night an airman lands on the island. It is ironic that the three boys get their wish of having an adult on the island, but not in the way that they expected.

Jack wants to hunt the new beast, but Ralph is less sure and admits that he is frightened.

Key quotation

'Jack smacked Piggy's head. Piggy's glasses flew off and tinkled on the rocks. Piggy cried out in terror'
(p. 75)

GRADE BOOSTER

It is important to explore the deeper interpretations of a theme, for example, Percival's fear of the beast from the sea is perhaps just the fear of the unknown. This fear of the unknown, and the savagery it provokes, is a theme of the novel.

Key quotation

'The rules...you're breaking the rules!'

'Who cares?'
(p. 99)

Jack almost gets his way but Ralph asks the boys again, 'Don't you all want to be rescued?' (p. 111) and they listen to him. The older boys set off to search the only part of the island they have not yet explored, with Jack leading the way.

Simon thinks of the beast as human but cannot bring himself to tell Ralph.

Ralph takes charge again. He sets off to climb the path round the rock and finds that Jack has come too.

Jack says that the rock would make a good castle, and that it even has fresh water.

Chapter 7 Shadows and tall trees

Summary

- The boys nearly catch a boar.
- The hunters show they can be savage to other boys.
- There is an expedition up the mountain.
- The dead airman is seen at night, which causes panic.

Commentary

Ralph notices how dirty he and the other boys have become and wishes he could look like his old self: 'Be sucking my thumb next–' (p. 120).

This reveals that he is still attached to civilisation – in contrast with the hunters, who are becoming wilder and more like primitive savages. Simon tells Ralph that he is sure Ralph will get home safely.

The boys become excited on a hunt and form a circle around Robert. They beat him and jab him with spears, and even Ralph joins in. At one point Jack suggests that they should use a littlun in the game and actually kill him. It is not clear whether he is joking.

The boys are becoming more savage each day.

Ralph asks Jack why he hates him so much.

Ralph suggests they wait until morning to go up the mountain but Jack says he is going now and challenges Ralph to join him. It is important that the expedition to find the beast takes place at night. In daylight what was actually on the mountain might well have been obvious to the older boys. It was Jack's idea to go up at night and it is Jack who causes much of the trouble that follows.

Jack and Roger are led up the mountain by Ralph and, just as he gets near to the body, the wind pulls the airman upright and Ralph looks straight into the rotting face of the corpse.

Chapter 8 Gift for the darkness

Summary

- The boys are told about the beast on the mountain.
- Jack leaves to set up his own tribe.
- The hunters kill a pig and leave its head on a stick.
- Jack invites the other boys to join him.
- Simon hears the Lord of the Flies.

Commentary

Jack blows the conch and brings the boys together. He lies to them, saying that Ralph is a coward and that he didn't go up the mountain with them. Jack accuses Ralph of not being a proper chief.

Jack asks the boys how many of them do not want Ralph as chief. He gets no response. Jack announces that he is no longer going to be part of 'Ralph's lot' and runs away, inviting anyone who wants to hunt to join him. Jack's question to the boys is a classic mistake. The boys are unlikely to challenge Ralph when he is in front of them. If Jack had simply said 'Who wants a powerful hunter like me as chief?' he might have been more successful.

Piggy suggests that the fire should be lit on the beach as it would give off smoke just the same.

Key quotation

'He's a coward himself.' (p. 138)

A group of the younger boys has attached itself to Jack and he is still intent on hunting pigs. He now thinks that if they leave some of the pig for the beast then it will not come after them.

The hunters find a group of pigs and wound a large sow. They follow her into the forest and kill her. Jack guts the sow and cuts off the head. He places the head on a stick as a gift for the beast. When Simon finds himself in the clearing he sees the head covered in a mass of flies and thinks of it as the 'Lord of the Flies'.

Back on the beach, Ralph admits to Piggy that he is scared that they will never be rescued. Jack and the hunters arrive, stealing burning sticks and running off. Jack announces that he and his hunters are living along the beach and that they 'hunt and feast and have fun' (p. 154). He invites others to join his 'tribe'.

The hunters now have painted faces and are smeared with blood. They are turning into savages in appearance and action, and Golding refers to them as such.

Jack says there is to be a feast and anyone who wants can come. Two of the hunters end his invitation with the words 'The Chief has spoken' (p. 155). The hunters are beginning to treat Jack like a king and there are elements of worship in the way they now behave towards him.

Ralph insists that fire is the way they will be rescued but begins to sound less convincing. The boys want meat and like the idea of playing at being hunters. There appears to be an ancient instinct in them that they do not fully understand but which is beginning to take hold of them.

Simon is still watching the pig's head on a stick. He imagines that it tells him that the beast is not something that can be hunted and killed. It says that the beast is part of him.

Chapter 9 A view to a death

Summary

Build critical skills

How does Golding mirror normal human life by presenting the boys in two separate tribes?

- A storm is gathering over the island.
- Simon finds the dead airman and realises what he is.
- Simon frees the airman's parachute lines.
- Jack holds a feast.
- The boys dance and chant.
- Simon is killed.
- The dead airman is blown out to sea.

Simon discovers that the beast is nothing more than a dead airman and he frees the parachute from the trees so that the body stops moving. It is important that it is Simon who finds out that the beast is simply a dead airman. Simon is seen as strange by the other boys and his rather distant nature marks him out as a victim for Jack and the hunters.

Key quotation

'Demoniac figures with faces of white and red and green rushed out howling'
(p. 154)

Ralph and Piggy visit Jack's feast and are given meat to eat. Ralph tries to assert himself as chief but Piggy warns him that there is going to be trouble. Ralph points out that there is a storm coming and that if the boys had listened to him they would now have shelters against the rain. At this, Jack leads the boys in a dance and they are soon all chanting their hunting chant. The hunters are in a circle and work themselves into a frenzy.

Key quotation

"*Fancy thinking the Beast was something you could hunt and kill!*" said the head…"*You knew, didn't you? I'm part of you?*"
(p. 158)

At this point Simon appears and tries to tell the boys that the beast is simply a dead airman. They are too worked up to listen and they surround him, drive him to the beach and kill him in a savage manner.

Both the airman and Simon are swept out to sea. This is symbolic: the beast has gone, and so has the only boy who really grasped that the beast is not a real creature but is in each of the boys. It also removes all proof of the violence. Piggy's body is also swept out to sea later on.

Key quotation

'demented but partly secure society.'
(p. 167)

The storm begins with a 'blink of bright light' and drops of rain. Within a few lines the 'blows of the thunder' are 'only just bearable'. The climax is heralded by a streak of lightning described as 'a blue-white scar', followed by another: 'Again the blue-white scar jagged above them' (p. 168). The scar suggests the violence that is about to explode. When it does, Golding simulates the confused frenzy of the moment from the boys' viewpoint.

The paragraphs from 'Towards midnight' (p. 169) to the end of the chapter create an entirely different atmosphere. This is the calm after the storm, and the washing out to sea of Simon's body is described in a very moving and mystical way, as if he is being taken to heaven by the 'strange, attendant creatures, with their fiery eyes and trailing vapours' (p. 170).

The parachute is caught by the wind and lifts the dead parachutist over the trees and down to the beach. The boys are panicked by this and scatter into the darkness. The parachutist is blown out to sea. The sea also takes Simon's body away from the island.

Chapter 10 The shell and the glasses

Summary

- Ralph and Piggy think about Simon's death.
- Jack sets up camp on the Castle Rock.
- Jack's tribe attacks Ralph and the other boys with him.
- Piggy's glasses are stolen by Jack.

Commentary

Ralph tries to discuss the death of Simon, which he describes as murder. Piggy tells him there was nothing they could do and that they were not really involved. Jack has set up camp on the Castle Rock. He is now acting as chief of his own tribe. Jack has had Wilfred tied up and has beaten him for some unknown crime.

Jack is now dressed and painted like a savage and gives orders without expecting to be questioned. He is behaving exactly as any all-powerful tribal leader might. He enjoys exercising authority and uses violence quite casually in order to ensure loyalty. He is also keen for the boys to believe in the beast, because he is the only one who can lead them in their fight against it as he says earlier: 'if there was a snake we'd hunt and kill it…' (p. 35).

Jack says that the beast cannot be killed and he resists attempts to link Simon's death to the defeat of the beast. Jack plans to steal fire from Ralph as he has no means to start a fire himself. Meanwhile, Ralph, Piggy, Sam and Eric are struggling to keep the fire alight. They are now prepared to admit that the fire has a dual purpose, both as a beacon for passing ships and as a comfort in the dark.

This second purpose has become increasingly important and Piggy has to remind Ralph that the fire means rescue.

Build critical skills

What do you suppose Golding is describing in the paragraphs from 'Towards midnight' (p. 169)? Why does he not make it more obvious exactly what is happening to Simon's body?

Key quotation

*'That was Simon….
That was murder.'*
(p. 172)

Build critical skills

How does Golding present Jack to suggest that he is becoming a tyrant and a ruthless dictator?

Key quotation

'This was the first time he had admitted the double function of the fire. Certainly one was to send up a beckoning column of smoke; but the other was to be a hearth now and a comfort until they slept.'
(p. 179)

While Ralph is dreaming of home, Jack leads an attack on the shelter, which collapses. After a confused fight in the darkness, Jack and his hunters make off with Piggy's glasses.

Chapter 11 Castle Rock

Summary

- Ralph and the three boys visit Jack.
- Ralph challenges Jack.
- Roger sends down a rock that kills Piggy.
- Sam and Eric are captured.
- The tribe attacks Ralph.

Commentary

Ralph says he would have given Jack fire but now it has been stolen from them. Piggy is practically blind without his glasses.

Piggy still thinks that appealing to Jack's sense of 'what's right' will work, so the four boys decide to go to see Jack.

There are now two very different forms of leadership on the island: Ralph wants to make life better for everyone and be rescued. Jack is turning more savage by the day, enjoying the power and freedom from civilised restraint that the absence of adults has given him.

Ralph, Piggy, Sam and Eric approach Castle Rock, hoping to reason with Jack. Jack appears from the forest and Ralph tells him he is a thief. The two fight and Sam and Eric are taken prisoner. In the excitement, Roger uses the lever to send the large rock crashing down on Piggy, knocking him off the causeway to the rocks far below. Piggy's body is swept out to sea.

The tribe attacks Ralph, who is wounded by a spear but manages to escape. Jack is furious that Sam and Eric came to him carrying spears and that they did not join his tribe.

The twins try to reason with him, but the chapter closes with Roger moving menacingly towards them.

Chapter 12 Cry of the hunters

Summary

- Ralph is alone in the forest.
- Jack hunts Ralph.
- The forest is set on fire.
- Ralph is chased to the beach.
- A naval officer appears on the beach.
- The boys are rescued.

Key quotation

'They blinded me. See?'
(p. 187)

Key quotation

'I'm going to that Jack Merridew an' tell him. I am.'
'You'll get hurt.'
'What can he do more than he has?'
(p. 189)

Key quotation

'The rock struck Piggy a glancing blow from chin to knee; the conch exploded into a thousand white fragments and ceased to exist.'
(p. 200)

Commentary

Ralph sees the pig's head, now reduced to a white skull still on its stick, and lashes out at it. His action can be seen as symbolic. In destroying the pig's head he has smashed the idea of giving offerings to the beast. Ralph still retains his sense of right and wrong.

Ralph sees Sam and Eric on top of the hill and approaches them. The twins tell Ralph that the tribe is going to hunt him in the morning, walking in a line across the island. It becomes apparent that the twins are even more afraid of Roger than of Jack. Although Jack is still the tribe's leader, Roger takes a sadistic pleasure in torture. In anticipation of catching Ralph, he has sharpened a stick at both ends, like the one used for the pig's head – a clear indication that he does not expect Ralph to live.

Ralph's hideout is discovered the next morning and Jack orders boulders to be pushed down on him. Jack has the undergrowth set alight in order to burn Ralph out. Ralph realises time is running out.

At the last point of the island that is not ablaze Ralph collapses on the beach where they had first set up camp. He looks up to find a naval officer who has come because of the smoke from the fire. The officer assumes that the boys are playing games and jokingly says, 'What have you been doing? Having a war or something?' (p. 223).

The officer is surprised that a group of British boys has not been more organised and responsible.

Ralph tries to explain that it started out like that, and the officer encouragingly refers to *The Coral Island*. This mention of Ballantyne's story, which shows ideal rather than realistic behaviour, takes us back to the seemingly innocent beginning of Golding's novel. It also reveals the limitations of the officer's thinking. Ralph breaks down in tears and the novel ends with the officer looking in embarrassment at the navy ship lying offshore, unable to cope with this very un-British display of emotion.

> **Key quotation**
>
> 'Ralph wept for the end of innocence, the darkness of man's heart, and the fall through the air of the true, wise friend called Piggy.'
> (p. 225)

The passage of time

Golding is deliberately vague about the timescale of the novel. Some events happen close together in time but days or even weeks might pass between other events.

Take the example of the dead parachutist. When he lands on the island he has obviously come from a plane that is shot down over the island. Although

> **Key quotation**
>
> 'The skull regarded Ralph like one who knows all the answers and won't tell.'
> (p. 205)

> **Key quotation**
>
> 'Roger advanced upon them as one wielding a nameless authority.'
> (p. 202)

> **Key quotation**
>
> 'You don't know Roger. He's a terror.'
> (p. 210)

> **Key quotation**
>
> 'I should have thought that a pack of British boys…would have been able to put up a better show than that'
> (p. 224)

> **Build critical skills**
>
> What is the message Golding is trying to convey by using the fire to force Ralph into the open when it is also the reason that the boys are rescued?

we are not told anything about how long he is there before Sam and Eric find him, by the time Ralph discovers the body it has 'the ruin of a face'. Of course this could be due to the body's being burnt as the plane exploded but it could equally be the result of its having rotted in the tropical heat. We do not know.

Think about how quickly the boys' clothes become torn and fall apart and how their hair grows long. How long does your hair take to grow? There are several examples of time passing quickly in the novel.

Timeline

Chapter	What happens	Timing
1	Ralph is made leader. The conch becomes a symbol of power.	The events of these chapters take place on the first day on the island after the crash.
2	One of the younger boys has seen a 'beastie'. The signal fire is lit on the mountain but gets out of control.	
3	Jack hunts while Ralph focuses on building shelters.	By now Jack has made a spear and is turning into a hunter. Ralph is building shelters. Some days or even weeks have passed.
4	A ship passes but the signal fire has gone out. Jack and Ralph argue and Piggy's glasses are broken in one eye. The hunters have killed a pig and there is a feast.	The boys have been on the island for some time and have got used to 'the slow swing from dawn to quick dusk'.
5	Fear of the beast grows. Ralph sees that order is breaking down. Jack defies Ralph and the conch.	Later the same day as Chapter 4.
6	The dead parachutist lands on the island. Sam and Eric hear the beast and report it.	Some time has passed. The morning Sam and Eric see the dead airman may be some time after the body lands, not the next day.
7	The hunters become more savage and the game gets dangerous. Jack and Ralph find the body and think it is the beast.	Enough time has passed since the start of Chapter 6 for the body of the airman to have decomposed
8	Jack sets up his own tribe. The pig's head is left as a gift to the beast. Simon has a vision of the Lord of the Flies.	Chapter 8 opens shortly after the discovery of the dead airman, probably the next day.
9	The storm breaks. Simon is killed. The airman is blown out to sea.	The storm has been developing for some time.

Chapter	What happens	Timing
10	Jack's tribe moves to Castle Rock. It attacks Ralph and his group and steals Piggy's glasses.	This chapter opens the morning after Simon's death.
11	Ralph's group visits Jack. Piggy is killed. The twins are captured.	Chapter 11 opens straight after the attack on the camp by Jack's tribe – Eric is still covered in blood.
12	Ralph is hunted. The island burns. The naval officer rescues the boys.	Shortly after Piggy's death. Ralph spends one night in hiding before the hunt begins. The naval officer arrives at the end of the day.

The structure of the novel

The structure of *Lord of the Flies* is a simple one, with the events being revealed in chronological order through a third person omniscient narrator.

Exposition takes place in Chapter 1 where we are introduced to the boys and their situation and learn just a little background information. The rising action begins where order starts to break down midway through Chapter 2 and the climax occurs when order breaks down completely and Jack seizes power. Both Piggy and the conch are destroyed. Falling action follows as Jack remains in power until the resolution which occurs when the fire brings the naval officer to the island and the boys are rescued and returned to society.

REVIEW YOUR LEARNING

(Answers are given on p. 99.)

1 What is used to light the fire?
2 What does the conch symbolise?
3 Which of the boys believes the beast comes from the sea?
4 Which boy finally discovers the true identity of the beast?
5 Where does Jack set up his new camp?
6 What methods does Jack use to hunt down Ralph?

GRADE *FOCUS*

Grade 5
To achieve Grade 5, students will show a clear and detailed understanding of the whole text and of the effects created by its structure.

Grade 8
To achieve Grade 8, students' responses will display a comprehensive understanding of explicit and implicit meanings in the text as a whole and will examine and evaluate the writer's use of structure in detail.

Characterisation

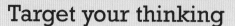

Target your thinking

- Who are the key characters in the novel? (**AO1**)
- How does Golding make his characters come to life? (**AO2**)
- What purposes are served by the characters? (**AO1, AO2**)
- What symbolic values might the different characters have? (**AO1, AO2, AO3**)

It is important to note when writing your answer that it is impossible to separate the author's use of characterisation from the themes of the novel. The examples given below integrate both characters and themes throughout.

Characters in the novel

Ralph

Golding intends us to see him as the central character and gives him a decidedly heroic appearance. He represents leadership and the values of civilisation.

He is physically attractive and has a natural air of authority. Ralph is fair-haired and stronger than the other boys, apart from Jack. In Chapter 1 Piggy looks at 'Ralph's golden body': his physical appearance is clearly a major factor in the other boys' seeing him as someone to follow.

There are early indications that Ralph is capable of at least limited cruelty. He cannot help himself from laughing at Piggy's school nickname and persists in calling him by the one name he has been asked not to use. Although Ralph is later capable of deciding between reason and instinct, he shows here that he certainly has this instinctive side to his personality.

Golding presents Ralph as quite childlike when he talks of his father. He refers to him as 'Daddy', which is quite informal in front of another boy, and he has a childlike faith in his father's powers.

Perhaps Golding has simplified the situation on the island by creating only two characters who are nearly adolescents, while the rest are obviously still children. This means that the issue of leadership is fought out as a straight contest between Ralph and Jack.

> **Key quotation**
>
> *'You could see now that he might make a boxer, as far as width and heaviness of shoulders went, but there was a mildness about his mouth and eyes that proclaimed no devil.'*
> (p. 5)

> **Key quotation**
>
> *'He's a commander in the Navy. When he gets leave he'll come and rescue us.'*
> (p. 8)

Perhaps because Ralph has his father as a role model, being in charge seems to come easily to him: 'he found he could talk fluently and explain what he had to say' (p. 30). It is significant that Golding has Ralph find the conch. Though the shell eventually loses its importance, Ralph discovers the means of summoning the others and of establishing order in the early days of life on the island. This is linked with the idea of his being a natural leader. At the suggestion that the group ought to have a chief, Ralph does not immediately put himself forward. He does not react strongly to Jack's insistence that he himself ought to be chief because of his former status but simply lets the boys decide for themselves. Golding suggests that Ralph is going to become a leader who values the opinions of others and who is likely to act in the best interests of the group.

Once the meetings start, he establishes himself as the boy to be listened to. He does not always know what to say, however, and often needs the help of Piggy to put into words what he is thinking. Ralph wants to organise the boys into building huts, keeping a supply of clean water and seeing that the fire is kept alight. Although Golding does not present Ralph as a natural thinker at the start of the novel, he clearly shows his development into someone who appreciates that thought is valuable. This is shown in Chapter 5 for example:

> Once more that evening Ralph had to adjust his values. Piggy could think. He could go step by step inside that fat head of his, only Piggy was no chief. But Piggy, for all his ludicrous body, had brains. Ralph was a specialist in thought now, and could recognize thought in another.

> (p. 83)

Ralph tries to be democratic even when dealing with the silliest things. For example he asks the boys to vote on whether or not the beast might be a ghost. This shows he lacks experience of being in authority. At times he falls back on the wishes of the group when he would do better to assert his own will.

For a time Ralph is able to control the boys by clever use of questions such as: 'don't any of you want to be rescued?' (p. 111), but he becomes frustrated when Jack begins to break away from the group.

▲ Ralph holding the conch in the 1990 film adaptation

Key quotation

'he was big enough to be a link with the adult world of authority' (p. 61)

Build critical skills

Ralph represents a type of authority. He would like to rule in the best interests of the group and would like the boys to behave reasonably. However, he is let down by this approach. Why do you think this is? What might Golding be suggesting here about people who govern in the way that Ralph does? Letting reason rule may be a good idea, but not all people are reasonable.

Key quotation

'The rules!...you're breaking the rules!'
(p. 99)

Key quotation

'Why do you hate me?'
(p. 129)

Key quotation

'I'm chief. I'll go. Don't argue.'
(p. 114)

Key quotation

'The air was heavy with unspoken knowledge.'
(p. 175)

Key quotation

'Inside the floating cloak he was tall, thin, and bony: and his hair was red beneath the black cap. His face was crumpled and freckled, and ugly without silliness.'
(p. 16)

In Chapter 7 Ralph thinks about the life he enjoyed in England. He finds it comforting to slip back into memories of his early childhood. In this way, Golding suggests that Ralph remains rooted in civilised society, while Jack adapts more readily to their new situation and exploits it for his own ends.

Primitive impulses are always there in Ralph, as they are in Jack and the other boys, but Ralph usually manages to control this side of his nature, thanks to his well-developed sense of morality.

Ralph and Jack challenge each other to feats of bravery in front of the other boys and Ralph shows he is as strong as Jack. It is Ralph who decides they should make the final trip to see what it is that Sam and Eric have spotted on the mountain and at this point Ralph is presented as very brave and clearly very strong-willed.

Once Jack has left and taken most of the boys with him, Ralph starts to lose power and status. He looks a pitiful character in Chapter 9, when he approaches Jack's camp for meat.

Ralph is involved in the killing of Simon. This shows that the primitive side of his nature is stronger than he realises: to some extent he is in denial rather than simply being in control.

However, Ralph understands what he has done and shows moral courage in not letting Piggy disguise the killing as an accident. He sees that the only hope for survival is to be rescued.

Ralph puts his faith in the adult world to save the boys. When he decides to visit Jack in Chapter 11 he insists that Piggy, Sam and Eric put on their school uniforms to show that 'we aren't savages' (p. 189).

Even when he is fighting with Jack he uses phrases such as 'You aren't playing the game'. Ralph's sense of British fair play is an important aspect of his character. These words from Chapter 11 sum up Ralph's attitude:

Key quotation

'Which is better, law and rescue, or hunting and breaking things up?'
(p. 200)

However, Ralph survives only because of the arrival of the naval officer. His ideas of fair play and decency would not have held out against the savagery of Jack and Roger.

Jack

Golding presents Jack as a contrast to Ralph and signals this initially through his very different physical appearance.

The colour black, which is often associated with evil or death, is symbolically important – Ralph is golden but Jack is dressed in a black cloak and hat. Jack also likes the whole business of dressing up and playing a part. From the first, he treats the choir as a private army and clearly thinks in aggressive, military terms.

Key quotation

'Choir! Stand still!'
(p. 16)

Build critical skills

What do you think is Golding's purpose in describing Jack as 'ugly' and Ralph as 'golden'? Do you think Golding believed you could judge from appearances?

Key quotation

'I ought to be chief… because I'm chapter chorister and head boy. I can sing C sharp.'
(p. 18)

The choir calls him by his surname, Merridew. This formal use of surnames was common in boys' schools of this time.

On Roger's suggestion in Chapter 1 that there should be a chief, Jack instantly declares that he should be chief. This remark shows he can be vain and that he does not always think clearly before speaking or acting. The ability to sing C sharp might be impressive in a choir but is not a useful talent for life on the island.

We see an early indication of Jack's bluntness when he tells Piggy not to accompany him, Ralph and Simon on a tour of the area in order to see whether they are on an island: '"We don't want you," said Jack, flatly' (p. 21).

His head is full of ideas of hunting and he thinks this will be enough 'until they fetch us' (p. 27). Golding reveals Jack's selfishness here and also his lack of ability to think very far ahead. He has no thought for the weaker members of the group and embodies the notion of survival of the fittest.

In Chapter 4 he paints his face and it is as though the child in Jack is replaced by a primitive hunter: 'The mask compelled them' (p. 67).

Key quotation

"Like in the war. You know – dazzle paint. Like things trying to look like something else.' (p. 66)

In the same chapter, Jack rejoices at killing the pig even though his hunters have let the fire go out and the boys have missed the chance to attract a passing ship. There is a mixture of the savage and the child in Jack and we see the child who likes to play gradually being replaced by the primitive hunter.

Jack increasingly combats Ralph's democratic rules.

There is something sinister in his desire to shut himself away in a fortress. Golding again uses contrast as he suggests that Jack wants to behave like a king or dictator who rules his domain from his castle and uses fear to control his subjects, whilst Ralph is presented as having a more democratic approach. .

He is presented as both violent and cruel. Jack leads the attack on Robert and uses his spear on the other boy, whipping the hunters into a frenzy and suggesting at the end of the attack that they should act the kill out properly.

▲ Jack confronts Ralph

Key quotation

'painted and garlanded, sat there like an idol.'
(p. 164)

Key quotation

'See? See? That's what you'll get! I meant that! There isn't a tribe for you any more! The conch is gone'
(p. 201)

Key quotation

'My auntie told me not to run...on account of my asthma...and I've been wearing specs since I was three.'
(p. 3)

Jack shows he can be devious when he claims that Ralph hadn't gone to the top of the mountain to find the beast (Chapter 8). When Jack decides to break away from the group his words are a strange mixture of strength and childishness (Chapter 8):

Key quotation

'I'm going off by myself. He can catch his own pigs. Anyone who wants to hunt when I do can come too.'
(p. 140)

Jack elects himself chief and finds that the others will do whatever he says – not a good thing, given Jack's tendency to be cruel. Jack has the idea of leaving a sacrifice for the beast and loves the bloodiness of the kill. He leaves the pig's head as an offering and so is indirectly responsible for the effect this has on Simon.

Chapter 9 has a strong image that shows Jack's power. Jack is standing at the feast giving orders to the other boys. He appears like a king or tribal chief.

In the eyes of the other boys, Jack is now more powerful than Ralph. The fact that he can bring them meat when Ralph can only talk of the fire and rescue gives him this power.

Even though Jack does not consciously set out to disturb Simon, it is Jack's actions that lead to Simon's death. Jack sets the pig's head on a stick and it is this that causes Simon to have his fit and then to come stumbling into the group of boys.

Jack uses the killing of Simon to increase his hold over the other boys. Golding shows us Jack's savage nature most clearly when he is facing Ralph in Chapter 11. Jack is quite prepared to kill Ralph and to destroy all order and civilisation.

The final hunt for Ralph results in a fire that will have destroyed all the food on the island. Jack does not think about this, because his sole interest is in killing Ralph. He represents irrationality, savagery and evil, but it is important to note that but for the arrival of the naval officer, he would have triumphed.

Piggy

Piggy is presented by Golding as a physically weak boy who is nevertheless highly intelligent. The first time he appears in the novel he tells Ralph about his asthma. He is overweight and finds the climate of the island especially difficult. Thus Golding establishes his vulnerability and perhaps hints that he may not survive.

We find out very early that Piggy, despite his intelligence, is also gullible (easily taken in) in terms of relationships. He tells Ralph that he doesn't want to be called Piggy. This is an obvious mistake and it is clear that he is not going to command respect from the other boys.

Build critical skills

It is important that Piggy is not physically strong and that he lacks leadership qualities so he cannot be leader. Why do you think Golding has chosen to make the most intelligent boy also one of the weakest?

It is significant that Piggy's glasses are used to light the fire, which gives him some importance – even to Jack. Piggy's short-sightedness helps to make him a figure of fun to the other boys, but his glasses can be seen as a symbol of his intellectual vision and of civilisation itself. As Piggy's glasses deteriorate, so does Piggy, and so do the fortunes of the boys.

Key quotation

"I got to have them specs. Now I only got one eye."
(p. 76)

As early as Chapter 2, unthinking behaviour by the group causes problems for Piggy. He is horrified that the boys have started a forest fire, as he realises it means the destruction of their wood supply.

Golding connects Piggy to the world of humans and human progress. Think about the number of times Piggy mentions human inventions such as clocks and radios. Golding's point is that the trappings of civilised life are of little use on the island. Piggy seems unable to fully grasp this.

It is important to realise that Piggy represents a particular type of person and way of doing things. Today, he might be referred to as 'a nerd'. Piggy is a thinker, capable of taking the rough ideas that Jack and Ralph have and shaping them into plans for action.

However, he does not naturally command attention. He repeats himself and sounds ridiculous – as in his repeated cries of 'I got the conch' (e.g. p. 172). Gradually, by association, his ideas sound ridiculous too.

Piggy instinctively seeks Ralph's protection from Jack's bullying. Gradually the two become closer and depend on each other.

Piggy's loyalty and his death

Golding maintains sympathy for Piggy because he remains loyal to Ralph until the very end. He has seen that Jack is nothing but a bully. It is reasonable to assume that Piggy has met boys such as Jack before. Even though Ralph teases Piggy, this is taken as normal behaviour. Piggy knows that without Ralph's protection he would be Jack's victim.

At the moment of his death Piggy is still holding up the conch suggesting his dogged belief in the power of social convention and order. He still seems to think that the early rule about the holder of the conch being allowed to speak will be respected by the likes of Roger. When Roger levers the boulder over the edge it kills Piggy and destroys the conch. Thus the voice and the symbol of reason are destroyed together. This is a particularly cowardly act, as Piggy poses no real threat to Jack or Roger. It is simply a case of the strong attacking the weak. With the death of Piggy, Ralph is alone. He has no one to advise him and the importance of Piggy's ability to think straight becomes ever clearer.

> **Build critical skills**
>
> Although the boys need Piggy's wisdom for their long-term survival, they cast him aside quite early on and he is unable to influence events on the island once Jack becomes powerful. What is Golding suggesting here about the value we place on brute strength and charisma as opposed to intelligence?

▲ Ralph with Piggy

Build critical skills

What do you think Golding is trying to suggest when the boys laugh at Piggy's treatment, despite the fact that he is a good thinker?

Explain what groups of society might be represented by the various characters in the novel. What is Golding trying to achieve ?

Key quotation

'In a year or two when the war's over they'll be travelling to Mars and back. I know there isn't no beast – not with claws and all that, I mean – but I know there isn't no fear, either.'
(p. 90)

Simon

Simon is an unusual character. The reader learns in Chapter 1 that he regularly faints:

Key quotation

'"He's always throwing a faint," said Merridew. "He did in Gib.; and Addis; and at matins over the precentor."'
(p. 16)

Here Golding depicts the typical reaction of children to anything unusual in others. Simon is looked upon as being odd because he suffers from something that the other boys do not understand. When we finally get to see how one of Simon's attacks affects him, it seems likely that he is suffering from some form of epilepsy and that he is not simply fainting. Simon is described as:

Key quotation

'a skinny, vivid little boy, with a glance coming up from under a hut of straight hair that hung down, black and coarse.'
(p. 20)

However, his eyes are very bright, and like Piggy's glasses, a symbol of vision and truth.

It is clear that he is no physical match for Ralph or Jack. Yet, in spite of his apparent weakness, he has a certain presence. This can be seen when Ralph decides that Simon should come with him and Jack to explore the island.

Simon is capable of having good practical ideas. He suggests they make a map on tree bark because there is no paper (Chapter 1). He is also a kind boy: when Piggy is accused in Chapter 2 of being useless, it is Simon who points out that Piggy's glasses were used to start the fire.

Simon is loyal to Ralph. He is the only boy who helps Ralph build the first shelters, but even Ralph finds Simon odd: 'he's funny' (p. 56).

Simon goes off on his own without warning. In Chapter 3 he leaves Ralph and Jack and goes into the forest. The young boys follow him and he finds them food. This image of Simon as a leader of the simple children and provider of food for them has clear parallels with the New Testament accounts of Jesus and his followers. Other biblical parallels involving Simon occur in the plot.

The account of his trip into the forest at the end of Chapter 3 is full of religious imagery, and Simon seems to have a mystical quality about him. However, he is quick to counter his involvement in the creation of the beast myth. When some of the small boys say they are worried about the beast, Simon admits that he has gone into the forest alone at night.

Simon makes the radical suggestion that the beast exists in the boys themselves – an idea that is too difficult for the other boys to grasp and that only makes them laugh at him. He is the only boy who is really aware of the dark side that each boy has and the only boy who understands the true nature of the beast. After Sam and Eric have seen the dead airman, only Simon thinks it is unlikely that there really is a beast.

In Chapter 6 Simon thinks there is an injured human on the mountain, and he is very nearly right. He has a much clearer insight into this question, and the boys' situation on the island as a whole, than the rest of the group. Golding thus conveys the idea that Simon sees things that the others do not see. Even though this is not really supernatural, it would seem that way to the boys.

Simon suggests that they should all climb the mountain and face the beast. His mystical side becomes very important in Chapter 8, when he watches the pig's head on the stick. He imagines the 'Lord of the Flies' speaking to him and telling him that he is a 'silly little boy'. The vision also tells him that he was right to think that the beast was part of him and the others. Again, note the biblical overtones in this scene (it parallels the story of Jesus being tempted by the devil in the wilderness).

Golding again uses foreshadowing when the final warning that Simon imagines turns out to be horribly appropriate. He imagines the beast saying: 'we shall do you. See? Jack and Roger and Maurice and Robert and Bill and Piggy and Ralph. Do you. See?' (p. 159)

Simon tells Ralph that he will get home safely. He does not include himself. Perhaps this is because he does not think he will get home safely and he has seen a premonition of Ralph's safe arrival home. This adds to the mystical qualities that surround Simon throughout the novel.

Simon also has much in common with the stories of saints who saw strange visions. Many saints were misunderstood and even persecuted

Build critical skills

Golding surrounds Simon with some of the most liturgic language in the novel but Simon is ultimately destroyed. What do you think he is saying about the role of religion in society?

Key quotation

'Simon became inarticulate in his effort to express mankind's essential illness. Inspiration came to him.

"What's the dirtiest thing there is?"'
(p. 96)

Key quotation

'I just think you'll get back all right.'
(p. 121)

for their unusual ideas. Even the name 'Simon' is the same as that of one of Christ's followers, Simon the Zealot, who was martyred: some stories have him crucified, others sawn in half. Simon mirrors his death closely. Like the Zealot, Simon is a visionary who can see beyond 'belief systems' to Golding's truth that good and evil exist within us and that the only beast we fear is the potential for evil inside us. He could also represent the most important of Christ's disciples. Simon was called 'Peter' by Jesus; the name Peter comes from the Latin word for rock. Simon Peter was the first pope and therefore the first leader of the Christian church.

Roger

Roger represents a kind of sadist who hurts and kills simply for the pleasure of it. Golding first signals Roger's true character in Chapter 4. Some of the smaller boys have built sandcastles and spent time decorating them with shells, flowers and stones. Roger comes out of the forest after watching the fire and immediately kicks the sandcastles over. He has no reason to do this; it is done simply out of badness.

Also in Chapter 4 we see Roger enjoying teasing Henry, a young boy. Roger throws stones all round Henry but hides behind a tree each time. Golding uses this incident to foreshadow the actual killing of Piggy with a boulder.

In the presence of Jack, who arrives following the teasing, Roger changes and becomes darker still.

Golding does not give many physical descriptions of Roger. He looks simply dark and brooding. Perhaps this might be a deliberate ploy to make Roger seem mysterious and threatening.

After the mock hunt in Chapter 7, Roger seems genuinely disappointed that the violence has not gone far enough and wishes they had a real pig to kill. Roger accompanies Ralph and Jack in the search for the beast. On this expedition he does not say much but is a brooding presence throughout.

In Chapter 8 it is Roger who helps to kill the pig and Golding again emphasises his cruel nature as is not done quickly: 'The spear moved forward inch by inch and the terrified squealing became a high-pitched scream' (p. 149).

Key quotation

'...unsociable remoteness into something forbidding.'
(Description of Roger, p. 63)

Key quotation

'Roger's arm was conditioned by a civilization that knew nothing of him and was in ruins.'
(p. 65)

Key quotation

'When Roger opened his eyes and saw him, a darker shadow crept beneath the swarthiness of his skin.'
(p. 65)

Key quotation

'High overhead, Roger, with a sense of delirious abandonment, leaned all his weight on the lever.'
(p. 200)

Build critical skills

Consider how Golding uses Roger as an evil agent that is present whenever any of the boys shows weakness. List instances of this from the novel.

A major milestone in the development of Roger's character comes in Chapter 10. He learns that Wilfred has been tied up by Jack and is going to be beaten. No one seems to know what Wilfred has done, but Roger sees this as an exciting opportunity.

This is the point at which Roger realises that power creates opportunities for terror. He has no real interest in the outcome of the terror but is simply fascinated by the idea of being able to hurt others without being stopped.

The most defining point in Roger's character comes in Chapter 11 when he kills Piggy. He is very excited by the fight between Ralph and Jack and feels the need to join in.

Key quotation

'Roger received this news as an illumination. He…sat still, assimilating the possibilities of irresponsible authority.'
(p. 176)

Key quotation

'Roger, uncommunicative by nature, said nothing. He offered no opinion on the beast nor told Ralph why he had chosen to come on this mad expedition.'
(pp. 132–33)

Roger can be seen to represent a part of human nature that is present in everyone. The rules of society cause most people to keep this side of their nature under control. Roger has no one to stop him so he goes much further than he could at home. He is an example of the evil side of human nature let loose.

The 'delirious abandonment' as he is about to murder Piggy is a development of the idea that Roger can have power without responsibility. He kills Piggy when there is absolutely no need. This is simply bullying carried as far as it can go. The final indication of his cruelty is the moment when he comes down from the cliff to look at what he has done to Piggy. Even Jack backs away from him because, as Golding describes:

Key quotation

'…Roger who carried death in his hands?'
(p. 218)

Key quotation

'The hangman's horror clung to him.'
(p. 202)

Not only has he killed Piggy but he wants to admire his handiwork.

It is Roger who terrifies Sam and Eric into joining Jack's tribe. When Ralph meets the twins in the final chapter Sam tells him: 'You don't know Roger. He's a terror' (p. 210). Finally, the twins tell Ralph that Roger has 'sharpened a stick at both ends' (p. 211). The significance of this is clear, as the last time this was done, the stick was put into the ground and used to display the pig's severed head. Golding shows us that even killing Ralph is not enough for Roger; he wants to be able to put Ralph's head on a stick.

Roger may be the only character who poses a threat to Jack:

Key quotation

'Roger advanced upon them as one wielding a nameless authority.'
(p. 202)

▲ The island burns

Why does Golding have Sam and Eric betray Ralph? Consider the possible parallels, such as in Nazi Germany, where people with no real sympathy for the Nazis were persuaded, by threats, to betray Jews or others regarded as enemies of the state. You may be able to think of examples closer to home.

Key quotation

'*Samneric were savages like the rest; Piggy was dead, and the conch smashed to powder.*'
(p. 207)

He barely misses barging into Jack, showing there is a possible threat present.

Samneric

The twins Sam and Eric, referred to in the novel as 'Samneric', represent the normally decent general public. They are loyal to Ralph until the final episode. They spot the dead airman but are too afraid to investigate and so help to build up the myth of the beast.

The twins are important as symbols of the kind of sensible follower that a leader such as Ralph would rely on. They are never persuaded by Jack's style of leadership and join his tribe only because they are threatened and tortured by Roger. Even so, their change of allegiance comes as a serious blow to Ralph.

It is particularly striking that, when Ralph is hunted by Jack in Chapter 12, it is Sam and Eric who betray his hiding place.

The other boys

Robert, Maurice, Percival and Henry are examples of the general population of the island. They are happy to follow Ralph to begin with. Some feel loyalty to Jack through the choir. In the end they are all won over by Jack's love of hunting or by his ability to frighten them into submission.

The main group of boys represents the general population of any society. The little ones are very easily persuaded and will go along with whichever leader makes them follow him. They change sides quickly and easily and often make poor decisions about who is right and who is wrong.

Golding uses the non-central characters to suggest the way in which ordinary people behave. He clearly feels that many people in society are easily led. Remember that he had just fought in a war against normal people who had followed a cruel and fanatical leader.

REVIEW YOUR LEARNING

(Answers are given on p. 99.)

1 What does Ralph's father do for a living?

2 How does Golding contrast Ralph and Jack through their physical appearance?

3 Which boy is linked with sainthood?

4 Which boy is responsible for the death of Piggy?

5 What might Roger represent on the island?

6 What is the role of the littluns in the novel and what might Golding's purpose be for including them?

GRADE *FOCUS*

Grade 5

To achieve Grade 5, students will develop a clear understanding of how and why Golding uses language, form and structure to create characters, supported by appropriate references to the text.

Grade 8

To achieve Grade 8, students will examine and evaluate the ways that Golding uses language, form and structure to create characters, supported by carefully chosen and well-integrated references to the text.

Themes

Target your thinking

- What is a theme? (**AO1**, **AO3**)
- What are the main themes in *Lord of the Flies*? (**AO1**, **AO3**)
- How does Golding present the themes? (**AO2**)
- How do these themes relate to the characters? (**AO1**, **AO2**, **AO3**)

A theme in a novel is an idea or group of ideas that the author explores. There is no absolutely correct way to define the themes in any novel, and in any interpretation of literary themes there is bound to be some overlap.

These are the main themes of *Lord of the Flies*:

- the nature of evil
- civilisation versus savagery
- survival of the fittest
- fear of the unknown
- humans and the natural world

The nature of evil

The novel is in many ways an examination of evil and of how evil exists within us all.

This is hinted at in the early stages of the novel when Ralph, a supposedly 'good' character tells the other boys Piggy's real name when specifically asked not to. He does not however understand until later that evil is perhaps part of human nature.

This evil emerges as the novel progresses and reflects Golding's interest in how people can move from being good to being evil. Many modern thinkers believe that no-one is born with an evil nature, but that they can become so through lack of nurture, for example through poverty, neglect or abuse.

This is an old question, of great interest to the Victorians, and writers such as Dickens explored it in depth. Take the character of Nancy in Oliver Twist, who has been brought up on the streets and sold into prostitution while still a child. Even with this awful upbringing she sacrifices herself to save young Oliver.

Roger represents the type of person who just needs a chance to let this evil run free. Golding leaves it open to the reader to decide why this is. We do not know what nurturing or lack of nurturing factors have made Jack and Roger the way they are.

The murder of Simon shows that even the boys who are good can be influenced to be evil. The key factor with Ralph and Piggy is their remorse for their part in the killing. Piggy tries to pretend it did not happen, but he is still sorry for Simon; Ralph talks about the incident and realises he has been part of something terrible.

There are forces acting on the boys that bring about changes in their characters. If there were a ready source of meat on the island then Jack would not become the savage hunter that he turns into. If the dead airman had not landed on the island then many of the fears about the beast would not have developed as far as they do. The novel traces the effects of such forces on different boys. There are real tests of character on the island. Some boys behave well under this pressure but others become cruel and primitive. The way in which different boys respond to pressure is a key feature of the novel.

Civilisation versus savagery

The novel explores the idea that there are circumstances in which any individual could become a primitive human being who is driven by instinct. The dark side of human nature is strong in both Jack and Roger and they are not able to control where this takes them. They revert to a much more primitive form of behaviour than that upheld by modern Western society. Golding is perhaps putting forward the idea that some people are more ready than others to let their primitive instincts rule them. Jack and the hunters become uncivilised in the wildest sense. However, almost all the boys come to follow Jack, other than those like Simon and Piggy who are destroyed by them and Ralph only survives through luck. This leaves readers with the less comforting notion that the savage instinct is not located in particular people but in us all.

At the start of the book the boys cling closely to things associated with their former life. They still wear their uniforms in spite of the heat. Jack still addresses the choir. Gradually these old ties to the adult world disappear. The boys' clothes fall apart and the hunters discard most of theirs and paint themselves instead. The pitting of huts against hunting is symbolic of the conflicting forces of civilisation versus savagery. The irony is that both are necessary for survival as we need both food and shelter.

Ralph tries to run the island in the way that a British adult would have done. The conch, the shelters, rules about where to take water from and where to go to the toilet are all aspects of this. It is true that Ralph's

Key quotation

'You were outside. Outside the circle. You never really came in. Didn't you see what we – what they did?'
(p. 173)

Build critical skills

Look at the end of Chapter 8 from '"You are a silly little boy," said the Lord of the Flies…' (pp. 157–59).

What does the Lord of the Flies say in this section about evil?

Why has Golding chosen Simon to be the only boy to hear this information? Explore how this impacts on the events of the rest of the novel.

Key quotation

'The world, that understandable and lawful world, was slipping away.'
(p. 98)

and Piggy's ideas would probably have resulted in the best life for the whole group. It is also likely that, if the fire had been kept going as Ralph wanted, then the boys would have been rescued by the first ship.

Because there are no adults to enforce the rules, the society on the island gradually falls apart. The reason and interest in the common good that Ralph shows is overpowered by the primitive side of human nature that emerges in Jack and the hunters.

At this stage Roger is still influenced by the rules of a civilised society, represented by parents, school, the police and the law but, by the end of the novel, this has been stripped away because none of these agencies is present on the island. Once the conch has been smashed, Piggy killed and the fire on the mountain quenched, even the symbolic representations of civilisation have disappeared and Roger can free the beast within him, without fear of recrimination. Golding shows that, if there is a threat to Jack as leader, it is Roger in his 'only just avoiding pushing' (p. 202) Jack out of the way in his advance upon Sam and Eric to show him the proper way to torture.

The end of the novel is significant with regard to this idea. It is an adult who comes to the rescue – an adult in authority. In the end the old world of rules and 'proper' behaviour returns to the lives of the boys. It is also significant that Golding does not tell us what happens to the boys once they are off the island. Would Jack have been punished? Would Roger have been made accountable? These questions are left unanswered. The novel is concerned with the closed world of the island and does not try to explain what society would have made of the boys' behaviour. The naval officer thinks that the boys have been playing a game. He does not realise how dangerous a game it has been. The adult world of rules cannot understand what the boys have been through.

Since Golding uses the phrase 'the darkness of man's heart' on the final page it is likely that Golding was familiar with the novel *Heart of Darkness* by Joseph Conrad (published 1902). Conrad's novel is about a civilised man's descent into savagery. The central character, Kurtz, has been strongly affected by living in a remote part of Africa and has become a savage himself. This was a concern at the time, when European countries ruled over large areas of the world and saw themselves as 'civilised' and many of the countries they governed as 'primitive'. The fear that a person could find the native way of life attractive and begin to adopt it was real. (The word 'native' in this context did not necessarily mean primitive: 'going native' usually meant adopting the style of dress of the locals, eating local food and following local customs, although even this was considered eccentric. Even in hot countries, in Africa or Asia, you would have seen the British dressed as they would have been at home.)

Key quotation

'Roger gathered a handful of stones and began to throw them. Yet there was a space round Henry… into which he dare not throw… Round the squatting child was the protection of parents and school and policemen and the law.' (pp. 64–65)

In *Lord of the Flies* Golding explores the same idea as Conrad but focuses entirely on the European side of the equation. There are no savages to 'corrupt' the English, as there are in Conrad's story. Ralph and Piggy try to remain civilised whereas Jack, Roger and their followers become like primitive savages. Keeping up appearances and trying to be very 'British' about everything is part of what drives Ralph.

Jack does not set out to become the wild savage that he eventually turns into. Rather, this happens in a series of small changes. Some of his behaviour might have been learned at school. For instance, he would have known that tribal people often painted themselves before a hunt or a battle. What he discovers on the island is that hunting is much more satisfactory if there is some ceremony attached to it. There is no need to dance or to develop rituals around the killing of a pig. This is something that comes from Jack himself.

Key quotation

'The officer...was moved and a little embarrassed. He turned away to give them time to pull themselves together'
(p. 225)

Key quotation

'Which is better, law and rescue, or hunting and breaking things up?'
(Ralph, p. 200)

▲ Primitive savages?

Survival of the fittest

Charles Darwin introduced this idea as part of his work on the way species develop through evolution. According to Darwin's theory, species of creatures adapt to their surroundings over time, leading to the huge variety we see in life on earth. The creatures that are best suited to their environment (the fittest) have a greater chance of survival than weaker creatures or those less well adapted to their surroundings.

Build critical skills

The writer, Primo Levi, stated that '… the fittest survived; the best all died'.

In the novel, how does Golding present the deaths of Piggy and Simon as well as the near death of Ralph? Does the 'fittest' mean the best in a moral sense or can it be, depending on the environment, the worst?

Examples from nature would be:

- In a nest, the strongest chicks attract the parents' attention the most effectively and so get the most food.
- Pups, kittens or cubs in a litter have to fight for food – the strongest ones get the most food while the weaker ones may die.

Darwin gave many examples, including species of birds that had lost the ability to fly because they had become adapted to a place where there were no predators. He put forward the theory that creatures naturally choose the strongest and most successful mates and that the characteristics that make them successful are passed on down the generations.

Golding uses the notion of survival of the fittest in the novel. Ralph is clearly the best leader in terms of running things in a 'civilised' British way. In reality, this counts for nothing in the face of Jack's brutality, which makes Jack appear to be well suited to survival on the island (for one thing, he is a good hunter). While Jack is suited to his surroundings, Ralph tries to change the surroundings to suit himself.

However, although Jack comes close to killing Ralph and almost shows brutality to be more successful here than reason, he finally sets the island on fire. Jack and the other boys might well have starved after the fire, as they would have burnt down all the fruit trees. In the end Jack turns out to be no more of a true survivor than Ralph. Jack's instincts make him the stronger of the two leaders in the circumstances, but his need to destroy would probably have led to disaster for all the boys.

Fear of the unknown

One of the forces driving the actions of the boys is fear. This begins with some of the small boys being frightened by the jungle creepers that hang from the trees. It quickly develops into a fear of a beast that lives in the sea and comes out at night.

Build critical skills

Golding does not allow Jack to win. You might feel that this is part of the message of the book: that brute force will not triumph over intelligence. However, Jack is only defeated by the chance arrival of the naval officer. Is the ending of the novel then ultimately pessimistic?

At the very point when the older boys are about to persuade the others that there is no beast, the dead airman confuses matters. Sam and Eric see the body on the mountain but do not investigate. Simon does find out what 'the beast' really is and cuts the cords from the rocks so that the wind can take the body away. Tragically, he is killed in the circle before he can explain the truth.

The beast in the novel is always referred to in naturalistic terms: it is a snake, it comes from the sea, it is a great ape. From the earliest records of humankind, cultures have taken images from the natural world in this way and created spirits, monsters, demons and gods. From the Egyptian animal gods to the Minotaur and the Christian devil, human societies tend to give their fears a solid form and a name.

Throughout human history religions have developed that help people to feel more secure in the world and less fearful. They have their own explanations of the mysterious things found in nature (such as birth, death, the seasons) and usually have elaborate rituals associated with them. Although a fully developed religion does not appear on the island, there are signs that the early stages of this are present.

GRADE BOOSTER

Golding ensures that the reader is ahead of the boys in knowing that there is no real beast on the island. It is important that we know more than the characters so that the novel does not become a mystery tale or a horror story. Showing an awareness of this narrative device when appropriate could gain high marks.

Humans and the natural world

The boys are provided with the perfect environment in which to survive. All they have to do is to make full use of the surroundings. At first they take delight in the fruit trees and nature really does seem to have given them all they need. The fact that there are pigs on the island causes conflict to arise. It is difficult to imagine Jack developing the same intense feelings about fruit picking.

Apart from one storm, on the night of Simon's death, even the weather is kind to the boys. They find it hot, but at least they do not have to worry about being cold at night. The natural surroundings could be said to be benign (meaning kind or forgiving). The boys need only to treat nature with respect and they will never go short of food.

The first fire destroys part of the island. This should be a warning to the boys but not all listen to it. Even with the knowledge that fire can devastate the island, Jack chooses to burn Ralph out.

Key quotation

'The flames, as though they were a kind of wild life, crept as a jaguar creeps on its belly towards a line of birch-like saplings'
(p. 44)

The bloodlust that rises in Jack is uncontrollable. In the hunt for Ralph, Jack effectively destroys the things that nature has given the boys. This is an important idea in the book, and you should be able to draw parallels with the world at the time the novel was written. You could also extend this to ways in which the book remains relevant today.

Build critical skills

How does Golding describe Simon's encounter with the beast in Chapter 8 (pp. 157–59)? What is he trying to show the reader in this section?

Key quotation

'Simon became inarticulate in his effort to express mankind's essential illness.'
(p. 96)

Build critical skills

The behaviour of the boys towards their environment can be seen as typical of the way that humans have mistreated the planet. This aspect has become more topical since the novel was written. What environmental message may Golding have been trying to put across in his narrative?

GRADE *FOCUS*

Grade 5

To achieve Grade 5, students will reveal a clear understanding of the key themes of the novel and how Golding uses language, form and structure to explore them, supported by appropriate references to the text.

Grade 8

To achieve Grade 8, students will be able to examine and evaluate the key themes of the novel, analysing the ways that Golding uses language, form and structure to explore them. Comments will be supported by carefully chosen and well-integrated references to the text.

REVIEW YOUR LEARNING

(Answers are given on p. 99.)

1 Name four key themes of the novel.
2 How does Golding show the reader that at first the boys cling to their former lives?
3 What phrase used by Golding near the end of the novel echoes the title of a story by Joseph Conrad?
4 Who first introduced the idea of the 'survival of the fittest'?
5 Why might a reader see the ending of the novel as pessimistic?
6 In what ways does the island first seem to be a kind of paradise?

Language, style and analysis

Target your thinking

- What are some of Golding's more typical language techniques? (**AO2**)
- How does Golding create atmospheric settings in the novel? (**AO2**)
- What use does Golding make of symbols in the novel? (**AO2**)

You will notice from the questions above that when analysing language and style, the Assessment Objective with which we are most concerned is AO2, which refers to the writer's methods and is usually highlighted in the exam question by the word 'how'. It is of vital importance since it is the means by which writers help to create our understanding of plot, character and themes.

Examiners report that AO2 is often the objective the most overlooked by students in the examination. For example, candidates who fail to address AO2 often write about the characters in a novel as if they were real people involved in real events rather than analysing them as 'constructs' or creations of the writer.

To succeed with AO2, you must deal effectively with the writer's use of language, form and structure. Turn to p. 17 for analysis of the structure of *Lord of the Flies*.

Style is the *way* that a writer expresses the ideas in the novel. When you write about style, you are showing that you understand an important fact: the author of a novel has numerous choices regarding the features and techniques they use.

Golding has made choices about the following features covered by the word 'style':

- the creation of setting and atmosphere
- the use of dialogue
- figurative and literal language
- symbolism

Setting and atmosphere

It is important to remember that Golding said he set out to write a realistic version of *The Coral Island*. This means that the setting has to be a deserted island. Golding has followed some of the conventions of the original novel by R. M. Ballantyne in giving the boys food and water and in making sure they cannot get off the island. However, one major difference between *Lord of the Flies* and *The Coral Island* is that the boys in Golding's novel never try to leave the island. There is no talk of building a raft or a boat. There is simply the idea of being rescued. This gives the setting of the island an added importance, because the boys must make do with what they have.

The island is described in some detail in Chapter 1. Golding stresses the lush nature of the vegetation as well as its peace and beauty. The leaves of the palm trees are 'green feathers' suggesting their form but also making them seem soft and gentle. The water is warm and 'the air was bright'. The boys have landed in a kind of fantasy of no adults and no rules.

The island seems to be a tropical one, as it is always warm and there is plenty of ripe fruit on the trees. However, Golding uses contrast as we begin to understand that heaven on earth can become hell on earth. The fruit upsets their stomachs, the creepers resemble snakes, the pleasant warmth becomes oppressive heat and the forest suggests eternal darkness. The first death when the fire gets out of control is a sobering moment, foreshadowing further deaths to come. Tension is gradually built up as the spectre of the beast gradually gains credibility and control in the boys' minds.

Golding at times uses **pathetic fallacy**. The main example of this is the storm that has been developing and which finally breaks at the time of Simon's death. The boys are affected by the weather and it is probably one of the reasons they get so carried away. You have only to think how uncomfortable you feel on a hot sticky day just before a thunderstorm to realise the impact the build-up to the storm has on the boys.

The boys inhabit two main parts of the island:

- The edge of the beach near the bathing pool: Ralph and his followers end up here.
- Castle Rock: Jack instinctively retreats into a fortress even though there is nothing on the island to harm him.

The island is an unusual shape: 'It was roughly boat-shaped: humped near this end with behind them the jumbled descent to the shore' (p. 26). Jack's castle is described as being almost detached from the rest of the island: 'There, where the island petered out in water, was another island; a rock, almost detached, standing like a fort, facing them across the green with one bold, pink bastion' (p. 26). Creating the island in this way allows Golding to develop the storyline of Jack taking his tribe off to Castle Rock. Making the island boat-shaped is perhaps a joke reference to *The Coral Island*, in which boats play a major role. It is also possible that Golding intended the shape to be symbolic, suggesting that the island itself contains the means of rescue or salvation – in a moral sense.

Pathetic fallacy: where a description of the weather reflects the mood of the scene or a character, for example: 'sun gazed down like an angry eye' (p. 60)

Build critical skills

Find two more examples of Golding's use of pathetic fallacy and explain the effect of his use of this technique.

Key quotation

'The silence of the forest was more oppressive than the heat.' (p. 49)

Features of the landscape include:

- the 'great platform of pink granite' that forms the diving board and a natural meeting place
- the lagoon that surrounds the island: this keeps the sea from the island and makes the boys even more cut off while also giving them somewhere to swim (in the bathing pool) and play
- the mountain: this is important because it is the obvious place to light a signal fire and it is also the place where the dead airman lands
- the Castle Rock: a harsh and unforgiving place reflecting Jack's brutality
- the mark or 'scar' left by the plane, indicating the flaw in paradise which is man

The contrasts between the safety of the beach, the menace of the forest and mountain, and the security of the castle give the writer scope to move the boys around the island to suit the purposes of the story.

The boys have been presented with a perfect island – their own Garden of Eden. Parallels with the story of the fall of Adam from God's favour in the book of Genesis in the Bible are valid here. The boys fear a mysterious beast that drives them to terrible deeds; in the book of Genesis, the beast that causes the trouble is the serpent. The paradise with which the boys have been presented turns into a nightmare landscape for Ralph as he tries to run and hide from Jack. This might represent a view of the way in which humankind has treated the planet.

Dialogue

The speech patterns of the boys are in keeping with Golding's idea of creating a realistic version of *The Coral Island* and come from his own experience of having taught boys like those in the novel.

Much of what the boys speak is the school 'slang' of the day including words such as 'waxy' (meaning very angry), 'wacco' and 'wizard', all of which might sound strange to school pupils today. The differences in the speech of the key characters reflect their different social and educational backgrounds. For example, in the first chapter Ralph's mostly Standard English contrasts noticeably with Piggy's non-Standard grammar.

Even though Jack's behaviour becomes more and more savage, his manner of speech does not really alter. This has the effect of making his actions seem even more terrible, as they are being carried out by a boy (a choirboy at that) who speaks Standard English and sounds like a young English gentleman.

Two of the words used throughout the novel give the reader an indication that the boys are not very mature. The words are 'chief' and 'tribe'. The boys would probably have heard these words used in history lessons or would associate

---

Key quotation

'The shore was fledged with palm trees...The ground beneath them was a bank covered with coarse grass...Behind this was the darkness of the forest proper' (p. 4)

Build critical skills

Look at the way Piggy speaks, e.g.

'Nobody don't know we're here. Your dad don't know, nobody don't know...' (p. 9)

'What's grown-ups goin' to think? Young Simon was murdered. And there was that other kid what had a mark on his face.' (p. 189)

What is the effect of Golding making him speak in this manner?

Build critical skills

The presentation of Simon's fit comes to us through his own confused eyes. We experience the strange visions and odd conversation along with Simon. How has Golding made this section effective for the reader?

them with cowboy-and-Indian films or adventure stories. When Jack turns into a chief, he is copying a child's idea of what a tribal chief would be like.

Golding does not use the technique of telling us what the different boys are thinking. The characters' own words reveal their thoughts and states of mind. The fact that Jack shouts 'Choir! Stand still!' (p. 16) tells us a great deal about him and the position he holds in the eyes of the choirboys.

Simon's confusion at the time of his hallucinations in front of the pig's head comes through from the confused conversation that he thinks he is having with the 'Lord of the Flies'. We do not need to be told that he is confused. It is clear from the fact that the Lord of the Flies speaks to Simon that he is in a disturbed state of mind. He imagines the pig's head speaking in the voice of a disapproving authority figure. However, note that 'waxy' is a schoolboy word, not one that a teacher would really use, showing that Simon's image of authority is itself a little childish and confused.

Figurative and literal language

Golding uses imagery densely throughout the novel. The term 'imagery' refers to the kinds of word pictures an author creates to help us imagine what is being described. It includes similes, metaphors and personification. Such use of imagery allows the reader to become more involved because the effects created are often so vivid and realistic but can also evoke strong feelings, for example in Chapter 1:

Key quotation

'The coral was scribbled in the sea as though a giant had bent down to reproduce the shape of the island in a flowing, chalk line but tired before he had finished.'
(p. 26)

This helps the reader visualise the way the coral follows the form of the island but is also linked to the way a child might see things. The act of tracing around an object but getting bored before the end is something a child might do. It reminds us of the youth and vulnerability of the boys as we see the shape through a child's eyes. It also suggests a kind of fairy tale simplicity, linking to the idea that the island is a place of enchantment.

Golding uses colour to suggest the exotic nature of the island:

'the lagoon was still as a mountain lake – blue of all shades and shadowy green and purple'

(p. 4)

Contrast is used as the boys shed their black and grey uniforms and paint their faces, a strong visual image of their assimilation.

Personification is also used to enhance the vibrancy of the island. For example:

> 'the fire thrust out a savage arm of heat that crinkled hair on the instant'
>
> (p. 41)

> 'the swell…seemed like the breathing of some stupendous creature…the sleeping leviathan breathed out'
>
> (pp. 114–15)

Sometimes the imagery is quite simple. The following metaphor describes how Ralph's thought process was so complicated that it was impossible for him to make any sense of what was happening. At every turn, he is thwarted in his ability to come up with a solution.

> 'He lost himself in a maze of thoughts…'
>
> (p. 81)

The pig's head on the stick is clearly an important image or manifestation of the hideous nature of evil – it gives the novel its title, *Lord of the Flies*. This title is also a reference to Beelzebub, one of Satan's henchmen. The image of a head being eaten by flies is disturbing anyway, but becomes even stronger when linked to the devil. The voice Simon hears seems to come from this head and reminds the reader that Satan is not to be found externally but is inside us all.

Language is sometimes used to reflect the viewpoint of the character. As Roger is about to kill Piggy we are told:

> 'Below him, Ralph was a shock of hair and Piggy a bag of fat'
>
> (p. 199)

This communicates to the reader Roger's lack of empathy as in common with many psychopaths, he dehumanises his victim before committing his violent act.

Most of the sentences in *Lord of the Flies* are simple or compound rather than long and complex. We see this particularly in the stark description of the moment of Piggy's death.

> 'His head opened and stuff came out and turned red.'
>
> (p. 201)

Sometimes sentence fragments are used, such as when Ralph is being hunted by Jack towards the end of the novel:

> 'Break the line.
> A tree.
> Hide, and let them pass.'
>
> (p. 218)

This technique creates tension as it suggests the urgency of Ralph's situation and allows the reader to feel Ralph's fear.

Build critical skills

'Nothing prospered but the flies who blackened their lord and made the spilt guts look like a heap of glistening coal.' (p. 160)

What is the effect of this short extract? How does Golding's use of imagery create these effects?

Golding also creates effects by adopting a more literal style. The highly detailed, quite factual and rational description of the dead airman at the start of Chapter 6 make it clear what the 'beast' really is and explains precisely how it appears to move: 'the figure sat, its helmeted head between its knees, held by a complication of lines.' (p. 104) This allows the reader to observe how the boys respond to the news of the 'beast' without having to work out what it actually is. Golding's choice of technique means that the reader's attention is focused on the boys and not on whether there really is a dangerous monster on the island. In addition, the rational language used here seems to belong to the adult world in contrast to the irrational fears of the boys.

Symbolism

A symbol is something that the author uses consistently to represent or 'stand for' something else, often, but not always, an abstract idea. There is also room for personal interpretation here: not all critics interpret a symbol in exactly the same way.

The whole of *Lord of the Flies* could be seen as symbolic. Golding uses the closed world of the island to represent the world outside. Each boy represents a type of person and we come to see that Golding is writing about mankind in general. The kinds of behaviour we see reflect the behaviour of groups of people in the wider world. There are characters in the novel and groups of people in life who:

- take delight in hurting the weak
- try to lead by example
- are intelligent but are not physically strong
- are physically strong but have few ideas

The conch

The boys use the conch as a symbol of power. It gives the holder the right to speak without interruption – at least at the start of the novel. Piggy has an idea of how a sound is made using the shell and this ancient form of trumpet comes to symbolise law and order. It is significant that Piggy is holding the conch when Roger sends the rock down on him: the last trace of order is smashed along with Piggy himself.

▲ Ralph blows the conch

Piggy's glasses

Piggy's glasses are useful in a practical way because they are used to light the fire. They also symbolise wisdom. When Jack steals them he gains the ability to light the fire but none of Piggy's cleverness. The glasses also represent a link to the old world of school and the adult way of doing things. The destruction and theft of the glasses is a significant event: initially just one lens is broken, showing that the boys are losing their civilised nature, then, when the glasses are taken, Piggy loses his sight completely, symbolising the end of clear-sightedness and the descent into instinct and savagery.

Fire

Golding's use of fire as a symbol is quite complex. Initially, it represents the boys' connection to civilisation. The signal fire is a symbol of hope; when the fire burns low it suggests that they are becoming less interested in returning home.

On the other hand, the fire can also be seen as a symbol of destruction. When the fire gets out of hand in Chapter 2, perhaps it represents the carelessness of mankind towards the environment, while the fire at the end suggests a complete regression to savagery as it sweeps through the island.

Light and darkness

During the day the island is bathed in light: 'The sand, trembling beneath the heat-haze' (p. 14) and 'They faced each other on the bright beach' (p. 55). In reality fair-skinned children would probably suffer badly from the intense sunlight. This is not the case in the novel: daytime is a time of safety, at least at the start of the novel.

The boys are happy during the day, but: 'When the sun sank, darkness dropped on the island like an extinguisher and soon the shelters were full of restlessness' (p. 61). Bad deeds mostly take place under cover of darkness or in darker areas such as the interior of the island. The forest is seen as particularly menacing.

> **Build critical skills**
>
> It is interesting to chart the movement and status of Piggy's glasses throughout the novel. How does their deterioration mirror that of the boys?

> **Build critical skills**
>
> In the Prometheus myth, fire represents power, as Prometheus steals fire from the Gods. How might you use this idea in terms of Jack stealing fire?

GRADE FOCUS

Grade 5

To achieve a Grade 5, students will show a clear appreciation of the methods Golding uses to create effects for the reader, supported by appropriate references to the text.

Grade 8

To achieve a Grade 8, students will explore and analyse the methods that Golding uses to create effects for the reader, supported by carefully chosen and well-integrated references to the text.

REVIEW YOUR LEARNING

(Answers are given on p.100.)

1 Name three techniques used by Golding to create powerful images.
2 How does Golding present Piggy's social background through his speech?
3 What do you understand by the term 'symbolism'?
4 How is fire used symbolically in the novel?
5 Name three important settings in the novel.
6 What might Piggy's glasses symbolise?

Tackling the exams

Target your thinking

- What sorts of questions will you have to answer?
- What is the best way to plan your answer?
- How can you improve your grade?
- What do you have to do to achieve the highest grade?

Your response to a question on *Lord of the Flies* will be assessed in a 'closed book' English Literature examination, which means that you are not allowed to take a copy of the text into the examination room. The different exam boards will test you in different ways, and it is vital that you know on which paper the twentieth-century novel will be, so that you can be well prepared on the day of the examination.

Whichever board you are studying, the following table explains which paper and section the novel appears in and gives you information about the sort of question you will face and how you will be assessed.

	AQA	Edexcel	Eduqas
Paper and section	Paper 2, Section A	Paper 1, Section B	Component (Paper) 2, Section A
Type of question	Single question with bullet points as guidance.	Single question with a quotation from the text as a starting point.	Extract-based question requiring a response to an aspect of an extract and to the novel as a whole.
Closed book?	Yes	Yes	Yes
Choice of question?	Yes: a choice of one from two	Yes: a choice of one from two	No
Paper and section length	Paper 2: 2 hours 15 minutes. Section A approximately 45 minutes.	Paper 1: 1 hour 45 mins. Section B 50 minutes.	Paper 2: 2 hours 30 minutes. Section A 45 minutes.
Percentage of whole grade	21% approximately	25%	20%
AOs assessed	AO1, AO2, AO3, AO4	AO1, AO3, AO4	AO1, AO2, AO4
Is AO4 (SPaG) assessed in this section?	Yes	Yes	Yes

Marking

The marking of your responses varies according to the board your school or you have chosen. Each exam board will have a slightly different mark scheme, consisting of a ladder of levels. The marks you achieve in each part of the examination will be converted to your final overall grade.

Grades are numbered from 1 to 9, with 9 being the highest.

It is important that you familiarise yourself with the relevant mark scheme(s) for your examination. After all, how can you do well unless you know exactly what is required?

Assessment Objectives for individual assessments are explained in the next section of the guide (see pp. 67–71).

Approaching the examination question

First impressions

First, read the whole question and make sure you understand exactly what the task requires you to do. It is very easy in the highly pressured atmosphere of the examination room to misread a question and this can be disastrous. Under no circumstances should you try to twist the question to the one that you have spent hours revising or the one that you did brilliantly on in your mock exam.

Are you being asked to think about how a character or theme is being presented or is it a description of a place? Make sure you know so that you will be able to sustain your focus later.

Look carefully at any bullet points you are given. They are there to help and guide you.

Of the three boards which offer *Lord of the Flies* only Eduqas has an extract-based question. For each board the wordings and formats of the questions are slightly different.

As a starting point, you may wish to underline key words in the question, such as 'how' to remind you to write about methods and any other words which you feel will help you to focus on answering the question you are being asked.

Below are examples of the question types from each exam board which have been underlined by students in this way.

Eduqas

You should use the extract below and your knowledge of the whole novel to answer this question.

Write about the character of <u>Ralph</u> and <u>how he is presented</u> throughout the novel.

In your response you should:

● refer to the <u>extract</u> and the <u>novel as a whole</u>;

● show your <u>understanding</u> of <u>characters and events</u> in the novel.

[40 marks]

[5 of this question's marks are allocated for accuracy in spelling, punctuation and the use of vocabulary and sentence structures.]

The shore was fledged with palm trees. These stood or leaned or reclined against the light and their green feathers were a hundred feet up in the air. The ground beneath them was a bank covered with coarse grass, torn everywhere by the upheavals of fallen trees, scattered with decaying coconuts and palm saplings. Behind this was the darkness of the forest proper and the open space of the scar. Ralph stood, one hand against a grey trunk, and screwed up his eyes against the shimmering water. Out there, perhaps a mile away, the white surf flicked on a coral reef, and beyond that the open sea was dark blue. Within the irregular arc of coral the lagoon was still as a mountain lake – blue of all shades and shadowy green and purple. The beach between the palm terrace and the water was a thin stick, endless apparently, for to Ralph's left the perspectives of palm and beach and water drew to a point at infinity; and always, almost visible, was the heat.

He jumped down from the terrace. The sand was thick over his black shoes and the heat hit him. He became conscious of the weight of clothes, kicked his shoes off fiercely and ripped off each stocking with its elastic garter in a single movement. Then he leapt back on the terrace, pulled off his shirt, and stood there among the skull-like coconuts with green shadows from the palms and the forest sliding over his skin. He undid the snake-clasp of his belt, lugged off his shorts and pants, and stood there naked, looking at the dazzling beach and the water.

He was old enough, twelve years and a few months, to have lost the prominent tummy of childhood and not yet old enough for adolescence to have made him awkward. You could see now that he might make a boxer, as far as width and heaviness of shoulders went, but there was a mildness about his mouth and eyes that proclaimed no devil. He patted the palm trunk softly, and, forced at last to believe in the reality of the island laughed delightedly again and stood on his head. He turned neatly on to his feet, jumped down to the beach, knelt and swept a double armful of sand into a pile against his chest. Then he sat back and looked at the water with bright, excited eyes.

AQA

How important is Roger in *Lord of the Flies*?

Write about:

- How Golding presents Roger in the novel
- How Golding uses Roger to express his ideas

[30 marks]

AO4 [4 marks]

Edexcel

'They walked along, two continents of experience and feeling, unable to communicate.'

How does Golding present the relationship between Ralph and Jack in the novel?

You **must** refer to the context of the novel in your answer.

[Total for Question 17 = 40 marks (includes 8 marks for the range of appropriate vocabulary and sentence structures, and accurate use of spelling and punctuation)]

Spot the differences

- AQA and Edexcel both have a choice of questions to answer.
- Edexcel uses a quotation from the text at the start of the question.
- Only Edexcel refers directly to 'context' in the question.
- Only Edexcel does not assess AO2 in this section.
- Only Eduqas gives an extract from the text.
- Only Eduqas does not assess AO3 in their question.

Important: Ensure that you include material that is relevant to the Assessment Objectives focused on by your chosen exam board.

Working with the text

If you are studying the Eduqas specification, read the passage again, underlining or highlighting any words or short phrases that you think might be related to the focus of the question and are of special interest. For example, the words or phrases might be surprising, unusual or amusing. You might have a strong emotional or analytical reaction to them or you might think that they are particularly clever or noteworthy.

These words or phrases may work together to produce a particular effect or to get you to think about a particular theme or to explore the methods the writer uses to present a character in a particular way for their own purposes. You may pick out examples of literary techniques such as lists or use of imagery, or sound effects such as alliteration or onomatopoeia.

You may spot an unusual word order, sentence construction or use of punctuation. The important thing to remember is that when you start writing you must try to explain the effects created by these words, phrases or techniques, and not simply identify what they mean. Above all, ensure that you are answering the question.

Planning your answer

It is advisable to write a brief plan to help you to gather and organise your thoughts before you start writing your response. This will stop you repeating yourself or getting into a muddle. A plan is not a first draft. You will not have time to do this. In fact, if your plan has any full sentences, you are probably eating into the time you have available for writing a really insightful and considered answer.

You may find it helpful to use a diagram of some sort – perhaps a spider diagram or flow chart. This may help you to keep your mind open to new ideas as you plan, so that you can slot them in. Arranging your thoughts then is a simple matter of numbering the branches in the best possible order. Or you could make a list instead. The important thing is to choose a method that works for *you*.

The other advantage of having a plan is that if you run out of time, the examiner can look at the plan and may be able to give you an extra mark or two based on what you were going to do next.

Writing your answer

Now you are ready to start writing your answer. The first thing to remember is that you are working against the clock and so it is really important to use your time wisely.

It is possible that you may not have time to deal with all of the points you wish to make in your response. If you are studying the Eduqas and AQA specifications it is important to remember that if you simply identify several language features and make a brief comment on each, you will be working at a fairly low level. The idea is to select the ones that you find most interesting and develop them in a sustained and detailed manner. In order to move up the levels in the mark scheme, it is important to write a lot about a little, rather than a little about a lot.

For all specifications you must also remember to address the whole question as you will be penalised if you fail to do so.

If you have any time left at the end of the examination, do not waste it. Check carefully that your meaning is clear and that you have done the very best that you can. Look back at your plan and check that you have included all your best points. Is there anything else you can add? Keep thinking until you are told to put your pen down.

Referring to the author and title

You can refer to Golding either by name (make sure you spell it correctly) or as 'the writer'. You should never use his first name (William) – this sounds as if you know him personally. You can also save time by giving the novel title in full the first time you refer to it, and afterwards simply referring to it as 'the novel'.

GRADE BOOSTER

Do not lose sight of the author in your essay. Remember that *Lord of the Flies* is a construct: the characters, their thoughts, their words, their actions have all been created by Golding so most of your points need to be about what Golding might have been trying to achieve. In explaining how his message is conveyed to you, for instance through an event, something about a character, use of symbolism, personification, irony and so on, don't forget to mention his name.
For example:

- Golding makes it clear that…
- It is evident from…that Golding is inviting the audience to consider…
- Here, the audience may well feel that Golding is suggesting…

However, remember this is not the case if you are entered for the Edexcel examination on this text as AO2 is not assessed.

Writing in an appropriate style

Remember that you are expected to write in a suitable register. This means that you need to use an appropriate style. This means:

- not using colloquial language or slang, e.g. 'Jack is a nasty piece of work. A bit of a toe-rag really.' (The only exception is when quoting from the text.)
- not becoming too personal, e.g. 'Ralph is like my mate, right, 'cos he…'
- using suitable phrases for an academic essay, e.g. 'It could be argued that', not 'I reckon that…'
- not being too dogmatic. Don't say 'This means that…' It is much better to say 'This might suggest that…'

When writing an answer for the Eduqas or AQA specification you are also expected to be able to use a range of technical terms correctly. However, if you can't remember the correct name for a technique but can describe the effect it creates, you should still go ahead and do so.

GRADE *BOOSTER*

When discussing language for AQA or Eduqas, if you can't decide whether a phrase is a simile or a metaphor, you can still refer to it as an example of imagery.

The first person ('I')

It is perfectly appropriate to say 'I feel' or 'I think'. Just remember that you are being asked for your opinion about *what* Golding may have been trying to convey in his novel (his themes and ideas) and *how* he does this (through characters, events, language, form and structure of the novel).

Spelling, punctuation and grammar (AO4)

Your spelling, punctuation and grammar are specifically targeted for assessment on this section of the examination for all three boards. You cannot afford to forget that you will demonstrate your grasp of the novel through the way you write, so take great care with this and don't be sloppy. If the examiner cannot understand what you are trying to say, he or she will not be able to give you credit for it.

How to raise your grade

The most important advice is to answer the question that is in front of you, and you need to start doing this straight away. When writing essays in other subjects, you may have been taught to write a lengthy, elegant introduction explaining what you are about to do. You have only a short time in the Literature examination, though, so it is best to get started as soon as you have gathered your thoughts together and made a brief plan.

Students often ask how long their answer should be. It is difficult to give a definitive answer because candidates have different-sized handwriting, but quality is always more important than quantity. A strongly focused answer of 2–3 pages that hits the criteria in the mark scheme will be rewarded at the very highest level. Conversely, a response that is 6–7 pages long but not focused on the question will not receive many marks at all.

Sometimes students go into panic mode because they do not know how to start. If you are studying the Eduqas specification it is fine to begin your response with the words, 'In this extract Golding presents...' because you need to start with the extract.

If you are answering an extract-based question for Eduqas, begin by picking out interesting words and phrases and unpicking or exploring them within the context or focus of the question. For example, if the question is about the way that civilisation is presented, you need to focus on picking out words and phrases to do with civilisation.

AQA and Eduqas have a strong focus on AO2: what methods has the writer used? Although there are a whole range of methods with which you need to be familiar, it might be something as simple as a powerful adjective. What do you think is the impact of that word? It might be that the word you are referring to has more than one meaning. If that is the case, the examiner will be impressed if you can discuss what the word means to you, but can also suggest other meanings.

For Eduqas, it is likely that you will find it easier to address AO2 (methods) when writing about the extract, as you have the actual words to hand. However, do not be tempted to quote at length from the extract. If you are doing the AQA specification, you will need to have memorised several useful quotations which demonstrate the writer's use of language. Use these, if they are relevant to the question, to help develop your answer. Do not use all the quotations you have memorised if they are not necessary to answer the question in front of you.

When writing for AQA or Eduqas decide whether there is a cumulative effect of a particular method. For instance, you may have noticed Golding's frequent use of metaphors which create intensely vivid impressions, so make a comment on the overall effect of his use of metaphors as well as analysing individual words.

For AQA and Edexcel you need to consider context (AO3). In other words, would Golding's readers view society differently? What might Golding have been trying to express about society through the novel?

Whichever board you are studying, when you answer the question you will need to respond to the whole text, not just one extract or moment. You *must* do this: you will be penalised if you do not.

Be careful to avoid lapsing into narrative or simply retelling the story. If you are asked about how Golding presents Jack, a question likely on the AQA or Eduqas examination, remember that the focus of the question is about the methods that Golding uses. Do not simply tell the examiner what Jack does or what he is like; this is a very common mistake.

GRADE **BOOSTER**

It is important to make the individual quotations you select brief and to try to *embed* them. This will save you time, enabling you to develop your points at greater depth and so raise your grade.

Key points to remember

- Do not just jump straight in. Spending time wisely in those first moments may gain you extra marks later.
- Write a brief plan.
- Remember to answer the question.
- Refer closely to *details* in the passage or from the text in your answer, support your comments, and remember you must refer to the novel as a whole.
- Use your time wisely. Try to leave a few minutes to look back over your work and check your spelling, punctuation and grammar, so that your meaning is clear and so that you know that you have done the very best that you can.
- Keep an eye on the clock.

GRADE FOCUS

Grade 5
- Candidates have a clear focus on the text and the task and are able to 'read between the lines'.
- Candidates develop a clear understanding of the ways in which writers use language, form and structure to create effects for the readers.
- Candidates use a range of detailed textual evidence to support comments.
- Candidates show understanding of the idea that both writers and readers may be influenced by where, when and why a text is produced.

Grade 8
- Candidates produce a consistently convincing, informed response to a range of meanings and ideas within the text.
- Candidates use ideas that are well-linked and will often build on one another.
- Candidates dig deep into the text, examining, exploring and evaluating writers' use of language, form and structure.
- Candidates carefully select finely judged textual references that are well integrated in order to support and develop responses to texts.
- Candidates show perceptive understanding of how contexts shape texts and responses to texts.

Achieving a Grade 9

To reach the very highest level you need to have thought about the novel more deeply and produce a response which is conceptualised, critical and exploratory at a deeper level. You might, for instance, challenge accepted critical views in evaluating whether the writer has always been successful.

If, for example, you think Golding set out to create sympathy for Piggy, how successful do you think he has been?

You may feel that the creation of sympathy for Piggy through the almost slow-motion nature of his death is too exaggerated and not shocking enough and if so, do you consider this a problem or not?

You need to make original points clearly and succinctly and convince the examiner that your viewpoint is really your own, and a valid one, with constant and careful reference to the text. This will be aided by the use of short and apposite (really relevant) quotations, skilfully embedded in your answer along the way (see 'Sample essays' on pp. 72–90).

REVIEW YOUR LEARNING

(Answers are given on p.100.)

1 On which paper is your *Lord of the Flies* question?
2 Can you take your copy of the novel into the exam?
3 Will you have a choice of questions?
4 How long do you have to answer the question?
5 What advice would you give to another student about using quotations?
6 Will you be assessed on spelling, punctuation and grammar in your response to *Lord of the Flies*?
7 Why is it important to plan your answer?
8 What should you do if you finish ahead of time?

Assessment Objectives and skills

All GCSE examinations are pinned to specific areas of learning that the examiners want to be sure the candidates have mastered. These are known as Assessment Objectives (AOs). If you are studying *Lord of the Flies* as an examination text for AQA, Edexcel or Eduqas, the examiner marking your exam response will be trying to give you marks, using the particular mark scheme for that board. However, all mark schemes are based on fulfilling the key AOs for English Literature.

Assessment Objectives

The Assessment Objectives that apply to your response to *Lord of the Flies* depend on the exam board.

AO1: AQA, Edexcel and Eduqas

> **AO1** Read, understand and respond to texts. Students should be able to:
> - maintain a critical style and develop an informed personal response
> - use textual references, including quotations, to support and illustrate interpretations

AO2: AQA and Eduqas

> **AO2** Analyse the language, form and structure used by a writer to create meanings and effects, using relevant subject terminology where appropriate.

AO3: AQA and Edexcel

> **AO3** Show understanding of the relationship between texts and the contexts in which they were written.

AO4: AQA, Edexcel and Eduqas

> **AO4** Use a range of vocabulary and sentence structures for clarity, purpose and effect, with accurate spelling and punctuation.

Skills

Let's break the Assessment Objectives down to see what they really mean.

> **AO1** Read, understand and respond to texts. Students should be able to:
> - maintain a critical style and develop an informed personal response
> - use textual references, including quotations, to support and illustrate interpretations

At its most basic level, this AO is about having a good grasp of what a text is about and being able to express an opinion about it within the context of the question. For example, if you were to say: 'The novel is about a group of naive boys stranded on an island' you would be beginning to address AO1 because you have made a personal response. An '**informed**' response refers to the basis on which you make that judgement. In other words, you need to show that you know the novel well enough to answer the question.

It is closely linked to the idea that you are also required to '**use textual references, including quotations, to support and illustrate interpretations**'. This means giving short direct quotations from the text.

For example, if you wanted to support the idea that Piggy was physically weak, you could use a direct quote to show this: 'I've been wearing specs since I was three' (p. 3). Alternatively, you can simply refer to details in the text in order to support your views. So you might say: 'Piggy is seen as weak by the other boys as we learn that he wears glasses.'

Generally speaking, most candidates find AO1 relatively easy. Usually, it is tackled well – if you answer the question you are asked, this Assessment Objective will probably take care of itself.

> **AO2** Analyse the language, form and structure used by a writer to create meanings and effects, using relevant subject terminology where appropriate.

AO2 is a different matter. Most examiners would probably agree that covering AO2 is a weakness for many candidates, particularly those students who only ever talk about the characters as if they were real people.

In simple terms, AO2 refers to the writer's methods and is often signposted in questions by the word 'how' or the phrase 'how does the writer present…'

'**Language**' refers to Golding's use of words. Remember that writers choose words very carefully in order to achieve particular effects. They may spend quite a long time deciding between two or three words which are similar in meaning in order to create the precise effect that they are looking for.

If you are addressing AO2 in your response to *Lord of the Flies,* you will typically find yourself using Golding's name and exploring the choices he has made. For example, if you say: 'Golding describes Jack as ugly without silliness' this will set you on the right path to explaining why his choice of words is interesting. It is this explanation that addresses AO2, while 'Jack was ugly without silliness' is a simple AO1 comment.

You may wish to explore why he describes Jack as ugly and how this ugliness not being silly impacts on our feelings towards him. It is this ugliness which makes him unattractive as a leader.

Look at the first description of Ralph. The author chooses to focus on parts of his face that make him look kind and calm. There are many other ways in which Golding could have made the point that Ralph is not naturally violent. He could simply have stated it. Instead the reader has to do a little detective work.

'**Language**' also encompasses a wide range of writer's methods, such as the use of different types of imagery, words that create sound effects, irony and so on. AO2 also refers to your use of '**subject terminology**'. This means that you should be able to use terms such as 'metaphor', 'alliteration' and 'hyperbole' with confidence and understanding. However, if you can't remember the term, don't despair – you can still gain marks for explaining the effects being created.

'**Form**' refers to the narrative viewpoint of the novel (see p. 53 in the 'Language, style and analysis' section) as well as to more general ideas about the kind or genre of text you are studying. In the case of *Lord of the Flies*, the form is determined partly by Golding's wish to write a realistic version of *The Coral Island*. The novel is divided up into twelve chapters. Each chapter title makes it clear what the chapter will be about. This form helps to show the gradual descent of the boys from civilisation to savagery in a clear, organised manner.

Other devices that link to form and structure are Ralph's flashbacks to home life and sections of the novel where two events are happening at the same time (Simon's experience with the Lord of the Flies in Chapter 8 is happening at the same time as Jack is setting up his own 'tribe').

'**Structure**' refers to how the novel has been shaped by the writer. This might include the narrative technique being used – in *Lord of the Flies* Golding uses the third-person narrator; the order of events and the effects created by it; and the way key events are juxtaposed. Remember, for example, that the novel begins and ends with a military conflict raging around the boys. They are transported into their own world by war and it is a warship that rescues them.

Effects of structure can also be seen in the writer's use of sentence lengths and word order (syntax).

Remember, if you do not address AO2 at all, it will be very difficult to achieve much higher than Grade 1, since you will not be answering the question.

> **AO3** Show understanding of the relationship between texts and the contexts in which they were written.

This applies to the AQA and Edexcel examinations only. If you are trying to display knowledge of this area, do not treat the English Literature exam as though it were history. For example, knowing that *Lord of the Flies* was written during the Cold War might help your understanding of themes, but you should not get sidetracked and start to write at length about post-war Europe. Your task is to write about the novel.

You have to show some understanding of the context in which Golding wrote the novel. So you have to understand, for example, that British schoolboys in the 1950s were genuinely taught to live by the same values that the boys in the novel start out with – decency, fair play and a sense that being British was very important because it meant that you were superior.

You also need to show an awareness that there may have been different interpretations of the text when it was written. For instance, readers in the 1950s will have seen the novel very differently from a reader today, as many of them will have had some direct contact with the Second World War and would have been able to relate directly to some of the events in the novel.

It is important to understand that context should not be 'bolted on' to your response for no good reason; you are writing about literature, not history.

> **AO4** Use a range of vocabulary and sentence structures for clarity, purpose and effect, with accurate spelling and punctuation.

AO4 is fairly self-explanatory and is assessed in your response to *Lord of the Flies*. A clear and well-written response should always be your aim. If your spelling is so bad or your grammar and lack of punctuation so confusing that the examiner cannot understand what you are trying to express, this will adversely affect your mark.

Similarly, although there are no marks awarded for good handwriting, and none taken away for untidiness or crossings-out, it is obviously important for the examiner to be able to read what you have written. If you believe your handwriting is so illegible that it may cause difficulties for the examiner, you need to speak to your school's examination officer in plenty of time before the exam. He or she may be able to arrange for you to have a scribe or to sit your examination using a computer.

What not to do

You will not gain many marks for:

- **Retelling the story.** You can be sure that the examiner marking your response knows the story inside out. A key feature of the lowest grades is 'retelling the story'. Don't do it.

- **Quoting long passages.** Remember, the point is that every reference and piece of quotation must serve a very specific point you are making. If you quote at length, the examiner will have to guess which bit of the quotation you mean to serve your point. Don't impose work on the examiner – be explicit about exactly which words you have found specific meaning in. Keep quotes short and smart.

- **Merely identifying literary devices.** You will never gain marks simply for identifying literary devices such as a simile or a use of pathetic fallacy. However, you will gain marks by identifying these features, exploring the reasons why you think the author has used them and offering a thoughtful consideration of how they might impact on readers, as well as an evaluation of how effective you think they are.

- **Giving unsubstantiated opinions.** The examiner will be keen to give you marks for your opinions, but only if they are supported by reasoned argument and references to the text.

- **Writing about characters as if they are real people.** It is important to remember that characters are constructs – the writer is responsible for what the characters do and say. Don't ignore the author!

REVIEW YOUR LEARNING

(Answers are given on p.100.)

1 What does AO1 assess?

2 What sort of material do you need to cover in order to successfully address AO2?

3 What do you understand by the term 'AO3'?

4 Why is AO4 important?

5 Which exam board specification are you following and what AOs should you be focusing on?

6 Is it a good idea to identify lots of literary devices?

Sample essays

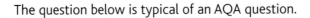

The question below is typical of an AQA question.

Question 1

What is the importance of Ralph in *Lord of the Flies*?

Write about:
- How Golding presents Ralph in the novel.
- How Golding uses Ralph to express his ideas.

[30 marks]

AO4 [4 marks]

You will see below extracts from exam responses from two students working at different levels. They cover much the same points. However, if you look carefully you will be able to see how Student Y takes similar material to that of Student X, but develops it further in order to achieve a higher grade.

In addressing the first bullet, both students begin by considering how Ralph's character is presented in the first chapter.

Student X, who is likely to achieve Grade 5, begins the response like this:

1 There are no marks for this kind of introduction. At this point the examiner may well be thinking 'Well get on with it, then'.

I am going to explain how Golding presents Ralph in the novel.

The first time Ralph is described makes an immediate impression on the reader. Ralph is described as 'the boy with fair hair' and the word 'fair' repeated several times to emphasise this. This makes him seem like a character we will find likeable.

2 Repetition is identified and some limited explanation is given to the effect of its usage here.

Ralph is also immature, reminding us that he is young as he stands on his head and grins at Piggy. This all makes him seem childish.

3 There is a general explanation on Ralph's childishness.

The way Ralph is described makes him seem quite athletic and we are told he looks like he could be a boxer, which tells us he is physically agile and he is also made to sound like a ballet dancer. He is able to move very easily and skilfully. Golding tries to make us see Ralph as strong, good looking and childish.

4 No technique is identified, but some comment is offered on the use of language.

We also have Ralph directly compared to something good when Golding writes: 'there was a mildness about his mouth and eyes that proclaimed no devil.' He is not a devil, so he must be the opposite.

5 A basic comment on language and the effect on the reader is implied.

Student Y, who is likely to achieve Grade 8, begins like this:

Golding begins the novel 'The boy with fair hair' giving an instant impression of Ralph's importance to the story as well as suggesting we are coming into the action in the middle as it progresses. The word 'fair' is cleverly repeated several times over the opening paragraphs contrasting with the dense foliage of the forest and the harsh-sounding nature of the creepers. Whilst they are in a place of danger and uncertainty, he stands out as a source of light.

1 Immediate explanation of effect created by the writer.

Golding reminds us of Ralph's immaturity, describing his behaviour: 'In the middle of the scar he stood on his head and grinned at the reversed fat boy.' He seems like an acrobat or a clown, there to entertain others as well as for his own amusement. 'Grinned' makes him seem like the Cheshire Cat, an almost comic image of someone at ease with what he is doing, but possibly a sinister sense of being superior to the fat, ugly looking Piggy. Whilst they are in a dangerous situation, he is able to still enjoy himself and, at this stage, there is still a sense of innocence in his character which will change as the novel progresses.

2 Original and exploratory point.

There is an athletic, balletic quality to Ralph's behaviour and appearance. We are told by the third-person narrator that 'he might make a boxer', telling us he is physically agile. He has strength and a powerful physical appearance, which marks him out from the other boys. This will later play an important role when the boys elect their chief. They want someone they like the look of and, compared to the 'ugly' Jack, Ralph is the perfect image of a good-looking leader. This may well be a comment

3 Explores Ralph's appearance and its significance later in the novel.

from Golding on the nature of how countries elect their leaders, something very appropriate in a post-Second World War society.

4 Explores the significance of Ralph with context in mind.

The description: 'He turned neatly on to his feet, jumped down to the beach' shows Ralph's agility, like a ballet dancer performing a well-rehearsed routine. There is a precision to the way the sentence is constructed, with the comma placed to show the break between the execution of actions. This further emphasises Ralph's control over his body and what he is doing. When contrasted with Piggy's total lack of physical prowess, this further emphasises his power.

5 Exploration of character and language.

Golding chooses to describe Ralph saying: 'there was a mildness about his mouth and eyes that proclaimed no devil.' The focus on mouth and eyes, shows there is a clarity of what may be going on in his mind, which can often be seen by how the eyes look and the mouth is the source of expression – the words we use and the feelings we have are emitted through the mouth. By focusing on these, Golding is saying that within Ralph is a goodness – he is not a devil. This is something which is vital when we later meet the evil-looking Jack who, in many ways, has many opposite qualities to Ralph.

6 Explores the ideas presented by Golding with a focus on the language used.

Both students then go on to consider the way that Golding presents Ralph when the boys are selecting their chief.

Student X writes:

Ralph shows good leadership qualities in the novel. He uses Piggy's ideas: it is Piggy who discovers the conch, for example, but can't blow it. Ralph blows it powerfully so that 'His ordinary voice sounded like a whisper after the harsh note of the conch.' There is a simile here which makes Ralph's voice sound small compared to the conch – showing the power of the conch as a tool for calling everyone together.

1 Identifies use of simile and some explanation of the effect, but could be explored more fully.

> Ralph has the advantage of being good looking and clever, Piggy is clever but not good looking and Jack is too. This is what helps ensure he is elected as the leader. Golding uses contrast cleverly when describing Piggy and his 'ass-thmar' and Jack's face being 'ugly without silliness' as this makes Ralph seem more appealing.
>
> When the actual issue of voting for a chief is discussed Jack assumes: 'I ought to be chief,' which shows his 'arrogance'. Golding wants us to dislike Jack at this stage.
>
> Golding lists the positive qualities of Ralph: 'there was a stillness about Ralph as he sat that marked him out: there was his size, and attractive appearance; and most obscurely, yet most powerfully, there was the conch.' By using the words 'obscurely' and 'powerfully' Golding is showing us that the importance of the conch in the decision-making process is great. The conch symbolises power and control, as it called the boys together and Ralph, the holder of the power, is therefore seen as the perfect leader.

2 Again, identifies and explains use of contrast, but could be explored more fully.

3 Aware of the author using language and character, but needs to keep the focus on Ralph.

4 Identifies listing but does not explain the effect.

5 Explanation of the effect of the conch and a symbol on the boys.

This is a promising start and would suggest that Student X is working at Grade 5 and is demonstrating 'clear understanding'. The response is well focused on the task and there is clear awareness of Golding's methods and their effects on the reader, though these are not always fully explained.

However, an even better response appears below. Student Y is working at Grade 8. Look carefully and see if you can identify the differences between the two responses.

Student Y writes:

> It is Ralph's leadership qualities which form part of Golding's message in the novel: a successful leader is able to use the positive elements of others close to them. Ralph is able to harness the knowledge that Piggy brings: it is Piggy who discovers the conch, for example, but cannot actually find a way to blow it. Piggy knows it will help call the others together,

but can't blow it, showing his physical weakness, but Ralph blows it powerfully so that 'His ordinary voice sounded like a whisper after the harsh note of the conch.' The use of the simile 'like a whisper' emphasises that the conch is so loud a normal voice sounds nothing compared to it. The word 'whisper' is almost onomatopoeic, a slightly hissing sound, which does not sound pleasant to the ear. The conch, however, booms powerfully: showing the huge power it possesses.

1 Detailed exploration of the author's ideas and use of language.

Golding describes Ralph as both good looking and clever. His main leadership rivals, Piggy and Jack, have obvious weaknesses, but we have not been shown any of Ralph's weaknesses yet. Golding does this deliberately to steer the reader into thinking that Ralph is the perfect leader. Both Piggy and Jack are clever but not good looking. This is what helps ensure Ralph is elected as the leader. Golding uses contrast cleverly when describing Piggy and his 'ass-thmar' and Jack's face being 'ugly without silliness' as this makes Ralph seem more appealing.

2 The explanation looks at the writer crafting the novel and ideas to guide the reader.

When the actual issue of voting for a chief is discussed Jack assumes: 'I ought to be chief,' which shows his 'arrogance' but also alienates him from the reader, who Golding intends to dislike Jack at this juncture. It is unlikely we are meant to like someone who simply assumes they should be in charge. Ralph makes no such assumptions and just sits there quietly, holding the conch. This contrast is used by Golding to show us the difference in the two boys: Jack is used to having his own way and controlling events, whilst Ralph is more reasonable and is always part of a democratic process.

3 Exploration of the differences in attitude between Jack and Ralph.

When Ralph is selected we are told: 'None of the boys could have found good reason for this' which shows us that the decision to select Ralph is an odd one. However, as readers we are less surprised, as the focus of the novel so far has been mainly on Ralph and Piggy. In fact, Ralph is the first

4 Looks at the writer's crafting of the whole chapter so far.

person we meet and Piggy has already shown us several reasons why he would be an unsuitable leader.

Golding lists the positive qualities of Ralph: 'there was a stillness about Ralph as he sat that marked him out: there was his size, and attractive appearance; and most obscurely, yet most powerfully, there was the conch.' The list of positives about Ralph are deliberate devices used by Golding to show us that Ralph has many positive qualities which make him the ideal choice. His selection is no fluke. The importance of his size and attractiveness are linked back to the 'adult world of authority' later in the novel showing that the boys still crave someone powerful looking to lead and guide them.

By using the words 'obscurely' and 'powerfully' Golding is showing us that the importance of the conch in the decision-making process is great. A leader needs something the group can identify with, whether it is an idea or a symbol. Here the conch symbolises power and control, as it called the boys together and Ralph, the holder of the power, is therefore seen as the perfect leader.

5 Explores the use of language and links it with the novel as a whole.

6 Explores the importance of the conch as a symbol.

This is clearly at a higher level and is beginning to consider Golding's methods in a thoughtful, developed style.

Both students then progress to write about why Ralph is the perfect choice of leader.

Student X writes:

When Ralph is selected he immediately demonstrates to us why he is the perfect choice. This is clever from Golding as it is a way of showing that the boys have not made a mistake, this is a person who will be a good leader. Initially he ensures that any rebellion from Jack is prevented by offering him a position of power: 'Ralph looked at him, eager to offer something. "The choir belongs to you, of course."'

1 Comments on the author's use of character and how he shows Ralph is a good leader.

2 Examines the effect of the word 'eager'.

Ralph wants to use Jack's positive qualities to everyone's advantage. The word 'eager' is a little childish, showing he really wants Jack to be involved and happy.

Golding presents a calmness about Ralph at this stage. "I've got to have time to think things out." He realises that leaders can't make sudden decisions, but have to be able to think. By saying this, Golding makes Ralph seem reasonable and calm, again showing us that this is a good choice of leader. He now has time to take stock of the situation and work out what they are going to do.

3 Another comment on character and how this is used to show good leadership.

Again, this answer shows some clear, sustained understanding, but there is room for improvement. It could be improved by giving some further detail on context as seen in the next section of Student Y's response.

Student Y writes:

When Ralph is selected he immediately demonstrates to us why he is the perfect choice. This is clever from Golding as it is a way of endorsing the decision just made by the boys: they have not made a mistake, this is a person who will be a good leader. Initially he ensures that any rebellion from Jack is prevented by offering him a position of power: 'Ralph looked at him, eager to offer something. "The choir belongs to you, of course."' It could be argued that Ralph is worried about Jack's dangerous nature, but this is unlikely as little of this has been revealed yet in the novel. It is more likely that he wants to harness the positive qualities that Jack has and use them to everyone's advantage. The word 'eager' is a little childish, showing it a bit of a game to him, but also shows he really wants Jack to be involved and happy.

All leaders need a strong group of supporters around them, whether this is their politicians or generals. In the context of the novel, a world that had been subjected to the harsh dictatorship of Hitler, Mussolini and Stalin would have been very

1 Explores the ideas and language in detail.

familiar with a leader who had strong men around him. Ralph is Golding's representation of a more democratic leader: he has been chosen by the people and then he chooses his closest allies. Sometimes an opponent needs to be given a powerful position so that he is not a threat – Jack, in this way, is kept happy by Ralph. This does not succeed in the long term and it is not long before there are arguments and a breakdown in agreement. Perhaps Golding is suggesting this form of government has shown to be less successful or that anyone with dictatorial leanings should be treated very carefully when it comes to politics. ←

2 Explores the context of the novel in relation to the leadership decisions made.

Golding presents a calmness about Ralph at this stage. 'I've got to have time to think things out.' He realises that leaders can't make sudden decisions, but have to be able to think. By saying this, Golding makes Ralph seem reasonable and calm, again reasserting that this is a good choice of leader. He now has time to take stock of the situation and work out what they are going to do. Again, this use of reasoning shows us that Golding views the perfect leader as someone who takes stock, does not make rash and quick decisions and tries to involve others in what they do. However, none of this takes into account the dangers of others and their way of thinking, something which the great democratic leaders in the 1930s discovered when Hitler's Germany invaded Poland. ←

3 Exploration of ideas with context in mind.

This response is convincing and there are signs of an exploratory approach. An essay continuing along these lines would certainly be achieving at the highest level, around a Grade 8.

When addressing the presentation of Ralph's voice of reason, Student X has this to say:

1 Aware of the writer creating an idea.

Ralph acts as a voice of reason and calm when there is chaos around him. Leaders need this ability and Golding shows that Ralph can be successful to an extent. However, Jack's dictatorial style becomes more powerful as the novel progresses. Ralph does not use fear as a way of keeping the boys together, but reasons with them and offers them safety: 'don't any of you want to be rescued?'. Jack finds another way of getting the boys under his control, by making them fear him and his 'tribe', getting the other boys to join them so that they are safe and not outsiders.

2 Uses a quotation but needs to examine it in more detail.

Golding may be saying that those in authority who use reason as a way of running a country will be less successful than those who rule by fear. Many countries have dictatorships who control the people completely. Jack rules this way.

3 Some examination of Golding's ideas but a little disjointed.

When Jack interrupts the person holding the conch, Ralph shouts: 'The rules!...you're breaking the rules!' By repeating the words 'the rules' we get a sense of their importance. The rules are vital 'Because the rules are the only thing we've got!' Golding is showing that Ralph's voice of reason is clear that there must be laws/rules that are followed. It is no use having rules if they are broken.

4 Examines uses of repetition.

Student X is showing an ability to achieve at Grade 5 with this clear, coherent response. The response never strays from the focus of the question and it is obvious that Student X has a solid grasp of the details of the novel as a whole.

Now look at the way Student Y approaches the presentation of Ralph.

Student Y writes:

Golding presents Ralph as a voice of reason and calm when there is chaos around him. By doing this he is showing the reader his view that leaders need this ability and Ralph can be successful to an extent. However, Jack's dictatorial style becomes more powerful as the novel progresses. Perhaps Golding is exploring how we are, by nature, drawn to more powerful people, or controlled by fear. This is certainly true when comparing the world Golding lived in, the post-World War 2 society, with the boys. Hitler's dictatorship was effective and all-conquering, but in the end the democratic, reasoned approach of Britain and the allied forces prevailed – but only just.

1 Insightful exploration of the context.

Ralph does not use fear as a way of keeping the boys together, but reasons with them and offers them safety: 'don't any of you want to be rescued?' (p. 111). Golding presents him as clever when he uses this tactic, as it reminds the weaker boys that he can offer them this hope – something Jack is not interested in. Golding uses this hope to show that we all cling on to the hope that something better will happen when we select our leaders – in this case they hope for rescue, or at other times there is the hope that the beast is not something threatening.

2 Exploration of the presentation of Ralph and how he uses hope.

When Jack interrupts the person holding the conch, Ralph shouts: 'The rules!...you're breaking the rules!' By repeating the words 'the rules' we get a sense of their importance. The use of the exclamation mark also shows that Ralph is determined to get his point across. The rules are vital 'Because the rules are the only thing we've got!' Golding is showing that Ralph's voice of reason is clear that there must be laws/rules that are followed. It is no use having rules if they are broken. However, if someone does not agree with the rules there will be problems, especially as there is no way of enforcing these rules. This is a problem on the island, as when Jack decides to break the rules, no one can stop him. Golding may be saying that those in authority who use reason as a way of running a country will be less successful than those who rule by fear. This can certainly be linked to the way Germany was ruled by fear in the 1930s, whilst Britain was a calm democracy. Many countries have dictatorships who control the people completely. Jack rules this way.

3 Insightful comments on language and ideas presented with a link to context.

Throughout the answer, Student Y sustains a convincing, thoughtful response which offers a range of interesting interpretations and which covers all the requirements to achieve Grade 8, and possibly higher.

Question 2

The following question is based on an extract and is typical of the format used by Eduqas.

> You should use the extract below and your knowledge of the whole novel to answer this question.
>
> Write about the characters of Ralph and Jack and how their relationship is presented throughout the novel.
>
> In your response you should:
>
> - refer to the extract and the novel as a whole;
> - show your understanding of characters and events in the novel.
>
> [40 marks]
>
> [5 of this question's marks are allocated for accuracy in spelling, punctuation and the use of vocabulary and sentence structures.]

Ralph turned.

"You could have had everyone when the shelters were finished. But you had to hunt–"

"We needed meat."

Jack stood up as he said this, the bloodied knife in his hand. The two boys faced each other. There was the brilliant world of hunting, tactics, fierce exhilaration, skill; and there was the world of longing and baffled commonsense. Jack transferred the knife to his left hand and smudged blood over his forehead as he pushed down the plastered hair.

Piggy began again.

"You didn't ought to have let that fire out. You said you'd keep the smoke going–"

This from Piggy, and the wails of agreement from some of the hunters, drove Jack to violence. The bolting look came into his blue eyes. He took a step, and able at last to hit someone, stuck his fist into Piggy's stomach. Piggy sat down with a grunt. Jack stood over him. His voice was vicious with humiliation.

"You would, would you? Fatty!"

Ralph made a step forward and Jack smacked Piggy's head. Piggy's glasses flew off and tinkled on the rocks. Piggy cried out in terror:

"My specs!"

He went crouching and feeling over the rocks but Simon, who got there first, found them for him. Passions beat about Simon on the mountain-top with awful wings.

"One side's broken."

Piggy grabbed and put on the glasses. He looked malevolently at Jack.

"I got to have them specs. Now I only got one eye. Jus' you wait–"

Jack made a move toward Piggy who scrambled away till a great rock lay between them. He thrust his head over the top and glared at Jack through his one flashing glass.

"Now I only got one eye. Just you wait–"

Jack mimicked the whine and scramble.

"Jus' you wait–yah!"

Piggy and the parody were so funny that the hunters began to laugh.

Jack felt encouraged. He went on scrambling and the laughter rose to a gale of hysteria. Unwillingly Ralph felt his lips twitch; he was angry with himself for giving way.

Student X, who is hoping to achieve Grade 5, begins like this:

1 Immediate focus on the question and the section.

Golding creates tension between the boys in this extract from the novel. There is a clear difference between Jack and Ralph and their attitudes towards what is important at this moment. This is shown by 'The two boys faced each other.' which shows a confrontation. They both have different ideals: 'There was the brilliant world of hunting, tactics, fierce exhilaration, skill; and there was the world of longing and baffled common sense.' There is a list of different ideals presented here by Golding. This shows how different their ideals are and how many there are.

2 Aware of the key issues presented in the passage.

3 Uses an important piece of the text as support.

4 Simple reference to writer's method.

While this is a steady opening paragraph which reveals some clear understanding of the extract, it is not yet demonstrating AO2 skills at the required level. Student X begins to address these skills in the second paragraph:

1 Appropriate use of detail.

2 Comment on the language chosen by Golding and its effect.

> Jack is presented holding a bloodied knife in the extract, 'Jack stood up as he said this, the bloodied knife in his hand' which makes him seem more dangerous and threatening – if as he has already used the knife to kill the pig, he won't hesitate to use it again. Ralph uses words, but Jack holds a knife which, to the reader, makes him dangerous.

3 Useful summary of the contrast in the boys' behaviour.

The response is certainly improving. Some of Golding's methods are considered in this paragraph as are the effects he creates on the reader. Although some points could be developed further, for example the focus on the description of Jack, the sense of a Grade 5 response is emerging. Student X now offers a further paragraph on the extract:

1 Identifies and comments on an event in the novel.

> Golding also presents the first show of violence from one of the boys to another. It is no surprise that this violence comes from Jack, as he is holding the knife, but thankfully he doesn't use it. The description 'The bolting look came into his blue eyes.' shows he suddenly loses his sense of control, making it seem as if he has a had a lightning strike inside. It moves him to hit Piggy, which shocks the other boys and the reader.

2 Use of appropriate textual support.

3 Examines the effect of the language on the reader.

By this stage Student X is close to a Grade 5, but now needs to move on to consider the whole novel.

First, however, consider this response to the extract by Student Y who is working at a higher level.

Student Y opens the response as follows:

> Golding creates great tension in this section of the novel, showing that there are problems which have been brewing for some time, between the older boys. There is a clear difference between Ralph and Jack

1 Clear sense of authorial purpose highlighted.

and their attitudes towards what is important at this moment. This is shown by 'The two boys faced each other.' showing a confrontation. By facing each other it seems they are equally powerful, not wishing to back down. Neither looks away, so there is a situation where tension rises not just for them, but for the other boys and the reader as well. Both boys stand for totally different ideals: 'There was the brilliant world of hunting, tactics, fierce exhilaration, skill; and there was the world of longing and baffled common sense.' Golding creates a list of different ideals. Jack's is full of emotive and powerful words such as 'exhilaration' and 'hunting' making him seem primitive. Ralph is more focused on things that are calmer and less active such as 'longing' for something to happen and a hope for 'common sense'. Words such as 'brilliant' associated with hunting show that, as a child, something like this is fabulous and exciting – we can see into the childish mind of Jack and his hunters. The word 'baffling' associated with 'common sense' again from a child's perspective means they can't fully understand what it is about common sense that should make it so important compared to fun things like hunting.

2 Effective use of textual detail.

3 Exploration of Golding's use of language.

This is a strong opening paragraph, focused on the task and showing clear understanding of Golding's methods and intentions. The response continues to focus on the extract:

Jack is presented holding a bloodied knife, which makes him seem more dangerous and threatening The choice of the word 'bloodied' makes it seem as if as he has already used the knife to kill the pig, he won't hesitate to use it again. Golding also narrates that 'Jack stood up as he said this' which adds power to holding the knife: not only is he holding a dangerous weapon which he has already used to kill, standing up puts him on the same level as Ralph and adds to the sense of menace and threat.

1 Uses embedded quotation.

2 Compared to Student X, this is a more developed and exploratory focus on the language and ideas that Golding presents here.

Throughout this section Ralph uses words to put across his ideas and feelings, but Jack holds a knife which, to the reader, makes him dangerous. This acts as a telling precursor to the violent act he is about to commit, so Golding is preparing the reader for this eventuality.

3 Explores the ideas presented in terms of what is about to happen.

By this stage Student Y has covered all the requirements for a Grade 6 and is moving into Grade 7. The next paragraph offered on the extract explores the actual moment of physical violence.

1 Exploration of the idea of violence presented here and in the novel overall.

Golding also presents the first show of violence from one of the boys to another, intending the reader to be shocked but not surprised by the actions of Jack at this moment. It is no surprise that this violence comes from Jack, as he is holding the knife, a symbol of violence and aggression. At this stage he is not willing to use it on another human, but this will change as the novel progresses and the boys become more savage. The description 'The bolting look came into his blue eyes.' shows he suddenly loses his sense of control with 'bolting' making it seem as if he has had a lightning strike inside and is now electrified by it into violent action. The word implies doing something quickly and here he acts before he has fully had time to think of the consequences of his actions. He is so incensed that what he has been doing, hunting for food, has not been well received, that he needs an outlet for all that anger – Piggy becomes the easy target and unfortunate victim.

2 Use of embedded quotation.

3 Compared with Student X, look at how this answer explores the language in greater detail.

Look at how Student X now considers the rest of the novel when examining the relationship between the two boys.

There has been a tension between the three boys from the start of the novel. Ralph laughs at Piggy's nickname in Chapter 1, 'Ralph shrieked with laughter. He jumped up. "Piggy! Piggy!"', and is only

1 Focus turns to the start of the novel.

too happy to tell the others. By repeating Piggy's name, Golding makes Ralph seem more immature and heartless for emphasising Piggy's weaknesses. Jack sees Piggy as physically weak and ugly and rejects him early on in the novel as well. Golding shows that the two strong boys see Piggy's weakness as a problem and also highlights their childish nature. Even the mature and gentle Ralph can be hurtful at times as he is just a boy.

The section where they first tell each other their names tells us something about the nature of their relationship. Jack is much more formal in the way he approaches names as he doesn't want to hear 'Kids' names...' Ralph is quick to digest this information and he realises 'This was the voice of one who knew his own mind.' This shows Ralph is intelligent. He tells the others of Piggy's name possibly because he is looking for attention.

'"He's not Fatty," cried Ralph, "his real name's Piggy!"' This is quite childish. The way Jack and the others react to this shows that they enjoy highlighting others' weaknesses which emphasises one of Golding's main themes: the survival of the fittest. Weak people will be laughed at and will have less chance of survival.

The relationship between the two boys becomes more strained as the novel carries on. In Chapter 11 Ralph and Piggy confront Jack and his new tribe after they have stolen Piggy's glasses to create their own fire. They are violent which shows they have become less civilised, 'Jack made a rush and stabbed at Ralph's chest with his spear.' Golding uses the word 'stabbed' to show this violence – Jack is not afraid to kill another person now. Golding makes him seem like a terrible leader, like Hitler or Mussolini in the Second World War.

The normally mild-mannered and rational Ralph now becomes angry and it seems the only way he can communicate back is with violence in both

2 Examines the effect of repetition.

3 Shows the effects of the writer's choice of behaviour for the boys.

4 Focuses on another section later in the same chapter.

5 Identifies a main theme of the novel and makes some comment on it.

6 Looks at a completely different section of the novel (Chapter 11).

7 Supporting quotation used.

8 Comments on what Golding is intending to do.

words and actions. This is showing how we can become violent if we need to: 'His temper broke. He screamed at Jack. "You're a beast and a swine and a bloody, bloody thief!"'

9 Another comment on Golding's intentions.

By using words like 'beast' and 'swine' he is using strong words for the time, showing how angry he is. The use of the word 'bloody' repeated twice, is probably the strongest swear word Ralph has in his vocabulary, so it is a sign of how angry and desperate he is at this point.

10 Comments on language and uses supporting examples.

Now read Student Y's response to the whole novel.

There has been a tension between the two boys from the start of the novel. Ralph laughs at Piggy's nickname in Chapter 1, 'Ralph shrieked with laughter. He jumped up. "Piggy! Piggy!"', and is only too happy to tell the others. By repeating Piggy's name, Golding makes Ralph seem more immature and heartless for emphasising Piggy's weaknesses. He should be mature enough to realise that Piggy is an easy target as a victim, but if the most moral and 'good' character in the novel can also reduce himself to this evil, petty nature, perhaps Golding is saying that this is something we are all capable of. We are all looking to feel better than other people – we all want to survive and be the best – a sense of survival of the fittest. Jack sees Piggy as physically weak and ugly and rejects him early on in the novel as well. This is ironic as Golding describes Jack is being 'ugly without silliness' – maybe Jack realises he is not physically attractive and tries to compensate for this by being powerful in other ways, possibly like Hitler did in 1930s Germany. His rule of fear has many similarities to Hitler's way of governing and controlling German citizens. Golding shows that the strong boys see Piggy's weakness as a problem and also highlights their childish nature. Even the mature and gentle Ralph can be hurtful at times as he is just a boy.

1 Focus turns to the start of the novel.

2 Examines the effect of repetition and explores in detail Golding's intentions.

3 Shows the effects of the writer's choice of behaviour for the boys and explores and analyses the possible meanings behind this.

4 Focuses on another section later in the same chapter.

The section where they first tell each other their names tells us something about the nature of their relationship. Jack is much more formal and adult in the way he approaches this matter of names as he doesn't want to hear 'Kids' names...' He is also trying to make his rivals feel inferior and this attitude somehow makes them seem immature and childish – one of Jack's many ploys to remain in control. Ralph is quick to digest this information and he realises 'This was the voice of one who knew his own mind.' This shows Ralph is intelligent and is able to adapt to the circumstances put in front of him. He tells the others of Piggy's name possibly because he is looking for attention, or to take away the embarrassment of Jack's comment on kid's names.

'"He's not Fatty," cried Ralph, "his real name's Piggy!"' This is all amusing, but quite childish. The way Jack and the others react to this shows that they enjoy highlighting others' weaknesses which emphasises one of Golding's main themes: the survival of the fittest. Anyone weak is seen as inferior and when all are trying to survive in a strange place, the weakest will fall first. Piggy is physically weaker, he looks ugly to the boys and his nickname is a source of fun for them. It makes the others feel more superior, gives Ralph a way of taking away negative attention from himself and is Golding's way of showing that we, as humans, have a natural need to feel more powerful than others, to ensure our own survival.

5 Identifies a main theme of the novel and explores ideas relating to it in some detail.

As the novel progresses the relationship between the two boys becomes more strained and divisions grow. This comes to a head in Chapter 11 when Ralph and Piggy confront Jack and his new tribe after they have stolen Piggy's glasses to create their own fire.

6 Looks at a completely different section of the novel (Chapter 11).

Mocking humour, which degenerated into physical violence has now further regressed to brutal confrontation, with spears. 'Jack made a rush and stabbed at Ralph's chest with his spear.' Words are

89

not strong enough as weapons anymore. Physical violence is the only way to communicate and Jack does this in many ways, whether it be torturing any troublemakers, using Roger as his general, or using the spear as a threat. The weapon shows that he means to cause injury and words such as 'rush' and 'stabbed' show the speed of his intention – he means to injure and kill. This shows the regression of the boys from civilised beings to savages and is Golding's way of highlighting the darkness inside us and the fact that, if left unchecked, we are capable of great evil.

7 Explores the meaning behind the use of violence at this stage of the novel.

Jack has moved on from using discussion as a way of deciding things and violence has become his tool of power. This could be Golding's way of linking his leadership qualities with those of a ruthless dictator like Hitler who used violence to control the German nation and quell any rebellion.

8 Evaluates Golding's intentions.

The level of exploration and detail in Student Y's response places this at a much higher level, covering most of the criteria for a Grade 8.

Top ten

As your examination will be 'closed book' and you will only have a short extract in front of you if you are studying the Eduqas specification, you might find it helpful to memorise some quotations to use in support of your points in the examination response. See the 'Tackling the exams' section on pp. 57–66 for further information about the format of the examination.

You don't need to remember long quotations; short quotes that you can embed into a sentence will be more effective. If all else fails, as long as you can remember the gist of what the quotation relates to, you can use a textual reference.

Top ten characterisation quotations

The following quotations can be used as a quick reminder of the way that Golding has presented the key characteristics of each of the main characters.

> **GRADE BOOSTER**
>
> If you find that you can't remember a full quotation, try and remember its main message. For example, in the first quotation below, you could just state that Ralph is compared to a boxer. You could then still use this idea to explain that perhaps Golding is suggesting that Ralph has powerful physical qualities whilst, at the same time, being mild mannered and benevolent.

Ralph

'You could see now that he might make a boxer, as far as width and heaviness of shoulders went, but there was a mildness about his mouth and eyes that proclaimed no devil.' (p. 5)

1

- Ralph is athletic, good-looking and a good person – the ideal leader.

'I'm frightened. Of us.' (p. 174)

2

- The short, sharp sentences emphasise Ralph's fear that the boys are more of a danger to themselves than anyone else.

3 'Ralph wept for the end of innocence, the darkness of man's heart, and the fall through the air of the true, wise friend called Piggy.' (p. 225)

- The list suggests there is much to weep for at the end of the novel: their civilised way of living has been brutally destroyed and things will never be the same.

Jack

4 Jack was 'tall, thin, and bony…his hair was red beneath the black cap. His face was…freckled, and ugly without silliness.' (p. 16)

- This negative description of Jack does not give the reader a positive first impression of him.

5 '"I ought to be chief," said Jack with simple arrogance, "because I'm chapter chorister and head boy. I can sing C sharp."' (p. 18)

- The word 'arrogance' is used to begin to create dislike in the reader.

6 '…he hadn't: because of the enormity of the knife descending and cutting into living flesh; because of the unbearable blood.' (p. 29)

- Jack is still innocent and placed in the dilemma of having to kill to survive. By killing he will break down the barrier between being just a boy and becoming something more dangerous and savage. He is scared of what this may mean to him and the others as he is giving in to his savage instincts.

GRADE BOOSTER

The memory part of your brain loves colour! Try copying these quotes out using different colours for different characters. You might organise them into mind maps or write them onto sticky notes and stick them around your room. Flash cards can also be fun and effective if you can enlist the help of a partner.

Piggy

'We're all drifting and things are going rotten. At home there was always a grown-up.' (p. 101)

7

- Piggy, forever the voice of reason, sums up what he feels has occurred since they arrived on the island. He regrets that they have regressed from civilisation and feels the need for a grown-up figure of authority before things get worse.

'The rock struck Piggy a glancing blow from chin to knee; the conch exploded into a thousand white fragments and ceased to exist.' (p. 200)

8

- The death of Piggy is significant as it represents the end of all order on the island. Now that he has been destroyed there is nothing to stop total animalistic chaos.

Simon

'Simon became inarticulate in his effort to express mankind's essential illness.' (p. 96)

9

- Golding uses Simon as a device to show the reader that we are the beast and nothing else. He is the only one who can see this.

Roger

'Roger's arm was conditioned by a civilization that knew nothing of him and was in ruins.' (p. 65)

10

- Golding emphasises that Roger's throwing of stones is governed by what he is told is right and wrong by parents. Now that society has gone he can, if he wishes, do what he wants, but he has not done this yet.

GRADE BOOSTER

The most frequently used method for learning quotations is to write them down, repeat them and then test yourself. However, if you are a visual learner, you might try drawing one of these quotes with the quotation as a caption.

Top ten thematic quotations

Good versus evil

1 'They knew very well why he hadn't: because of the enormity of the knife descending and cutting into living flesh; because of the unbearable blood.' (p. 29)

- The alliteration on the 'b' sound emphasises the massiveness of the decision to actually kill something.

2 'Demoniac figures with faces of white and red and green rushed out howling' (p. 154)

- Golding uses a horrifying image of demons to suggest the boys have become like devils.

Survival of the fittest

3 'Life became a race with the fire and the boys scattered through the upper forest.' (p. 41)

- The metaphor emphasises the danger the boys are in as they are chased by the fire.

Rules and society

4 'They walked along, two continents of experience and feeling, unable to communicate.' (p. 56)

- Golding uses the metaphor 'continents' to show that Ralph and Jack are both powerful figures, but unable to operate together.

5 'You were outside. Outside the circle. You never really came in. Didn't you see what we – what they did?' (Ralph to Piggy, p. 173)

- The repetition of 'outside' shows the worry about being an outsider.

6 'What did it mean? A stick sharpened at both ends. What was there in that?' (p. 212)

- Ralph is being hunted by the boys in the final chapter and the stick symbolises the end of civilised behaviour on the island.

'I should have thought that a pack of British boys – you're all British, aren't you? – would have been able to put up a better show than that' (p. 224)

7

- The officer repeats 'British' to emphasise that they have a clear identity and therefore are expected to behave in a certain, dignified manner.

Fear of the beast

'He says he saw the beastie, the snake-thing, and will it come back tonight?' (p. 35)

8

- The fear is emphasised by the use of the word 'snake' which makes it seem sly and dangerous to the boys.

Humans and nature

'Kill the pig! Cut his throat! Kill the pig! Bash him in!' (p.125)

9

- The four-phrase chant, with four exclamation marks, emphasises the lack of civilised behaviour that is developing in the boys.

'they had outwitted a living thing, imposed their will upon it, taken away its life like a long satisfying drink.' (p. 74)

10

- The use of this list shows the power of killing a living being, which Jack now recognises as a huge step.

GRADE BOOSTER

```
Another useful method is to record quotations onto
your media device and play them over and over. Or you
might try watching one of the film adaptations to spot
where a quote appears. This can be an effective method
as you have both sound and vision to help you, and you
can see the quotation in context.
```

Top ten symbolic quotations

The conch

1 'We can use this to call the others. Have a meeting. They'll come when they hear us–' (p. 12)

- The conch symbolises order and is used as a device by Ralph to keep order and call meetings.

2 'The rock struck Piggy a glancing blow from chin to knee; the conch exploded into a thousand white fragments and ceased to exist.'

- The death of Piggy and the destruction of the conch is significant as it represents the end of all order in the island. Piggy can be seen as the voice of reason and the conch was used to create order. Now they have both been destroyed there is nothing to stop animalistic chaos.

The fire

3 'There's another thing. We can help them to find us. If a ship comes near the island they may not notice us. So we must make smoke on top of the mountain. We must make a fire.' (p. 37)

- The fire is significant as it is used for many purposes, one being to enable smoke to be seen from sea so they can be rescued.

4 'This was the first time he had admitted the double function of the fire. Certainly one was to send up a beckoning column of smoke; but the other was to be a hearth now and a comfort until they slept.' (p. 179)

- Golding uses words like 'beckoning' to personify the fire and make it sound as if it is asking people to come to the island to rescue them.

5 'The flames, as though they were a kind of wild life, crept as a jaguar creeps on its belly towards a line of birch-like saplings' (p. 44)

- The simile makes the fire seem powerful, quick and destructive.

The beast

6 'He says the beastie came in the dark.' (p. 35)

- The beast takes on many forms – one is as a snake and another a monster. These make it seem dangerous and evil.

'There isn't anyone to help you. Only me. And I'm the Beast...Fancy thinking the Beast was something you could hunt and kill!...You knew, didn't you? I'm part of you? Close, close, close! I'm the reason why it's no go? Why things are the way they are?' (p. 158)

7

- Golding personifies the beast as a pig's head talking to Simon, who is the only one who hears it and understands what it really is.

"What I mean is...maybe it's only us." (p. 96)

8

- Simon ponders what the beast actually is and declares that he thinks it is just the boys themselves.

The mask

'the mask was a thing on its own, behind which Jack hid, liberated from shame and self-consciousness.' (p. 66)

9

- Golding presents Jack behind this disguise, almost like an actor, which allows him to do anything he wants.

Piggy's glasses

'I got to have them specs. Now I only got one eye.' (p. 76)

10

- Piggy's glasses represent being able to see clearly. Once one lens is destroyed, this symbolises the degeneration of the boys into savagery as their vision is collectively impaired.

Wider reading

Fiction

- Conrad, Joseph (1899) *Heart of Darkness,* Penguin Classics.
- McEwan, Ian (1978) *The Cement Garden,* Vintage Blue.
- Ballantyne, R. M. (1858) *The Coral Island: A Tale of the Pacific Ocean,* CreateSpace Independent Publishing Platform.
- Heinlein, Robert A. (1955) *Tunnel in the Sky,* SFBC. This book presents an opposite view of human nature, where stranded youngsters create the beginnings of a stable society.

Non-fiction

- Carey, John (2010) *William Golding: The Man who Wrote* Lord of the Flies, Faber and Faber.

Useful websites

- www.william-golding.co.uk – useful website with information about the writer, as well as the novel and his other works.
- www.william-golding.co.uk/life/reminiscences.aspx – extracts from *Scenes From a Life*, Golding's account of his early childhood.
- www.bbc.co.uk/schools/gcsebitesize/english_literature/ proselordflies – the BBC website contains some useful contextual information on the novel.
- education.cambridge.org/uk/whats-new/blog/posts/2014/09/ things-to-do-with-lord-of-the-flies – some activities to help you develop a further understanding about the novel.
- prezi.com/tybxkyr-wubi/the-coral-island-goldings-inspiration-for-lord-of-the-flies – an interesting presentation that compares *The Coral Island* with *Lord of the Flies*.
- www.historic-uk.com/CultureUK/schooldays-in-the-1950s-1960s – a useful site that comments on the life of schoolchildren in the 1950s and 1960s.
- news.bbc.co.uk/1/hi/magazine/6687549.stm – another site that has information on school life in the 1950s.

Film versions

- *Lord of the Flies* (1963), directed by Peter Brook.
- *Alkitrang dugo* (1976), a Filipino film, with female cast members.
- *Lord of the Flies* (1990), directed by Harry Hook.
- *Devolved* (2010), written and directed by John Cregan.

Answers

Answers to the 'Review your learning' sections.

Context (p. 16)

1   The context of a novel is the social, historical and literary factors likely to have influenced the author in writing it.
2   *The Coral Island* by R. M. Ballantyne
3   As a schoolteacher he saw at first hand how boys behaved.
4   An allegory is a simple story with a deeper meaning, designed to teach a moral lesson. In this case, the boys represent certain kinds of people.
5   His military service in the Second World War.
6   They begin by clinging to the rules and practices with which they are familiar but order soon begins to break down.

Plot and structure (p. 29)

1   Piggy's glasses.
2   Law and order.
3   Percival.
4   Simon.
5   Castle Rock.
6   Jack sets fire to the undergrowth to smoke him out.

Characterisation (p. 41)

1   Ralph's father is a naval commander.
2   Ralph is described as 'fair' and 'golden' whereas Jack wears a black cloak and cap and is described as 'ugly'.
3   Simon.
4   Roger.
5   Roger is a kind of sadist – one who enjoys inflicting pain on others.
6   The littluns might represent the easily led members of the general public who become gullible followers.

Themes (p. 48)

1   The nature of evil; civilisation versus savagery; fear of the unknown; survival of the fittest; humans and the natural world.
2   They continue to wear their choir uniforms.
3   The phrase is 'the darkness of man's heart' which is close to Conrad's title *Heart of Darkness*.

4 Charles Darwin in his groundbreaking theory of evolution.

5 Ralph is only saved from death by the chance arrival of the naval officer.

6 The island is tropical with warm weather, plentiful food and water and no adults!

Language, style and analysis (p. 56)

1 Similes, metaphors and personification

2 Through Piggy's use of non-Standard English

3 Symbolism is the use of an object, person or place to represent another thing or idea.

4 Fire begins as a symbol of hope but later seems to represent destruction and the descent into savagery.

5 Any three of these settings: Castle Rock; the mountain; the platform; the lagoon; the forest.

6 Wisdom and clear-sightedness.

Tackling the exams (p. 66)

1 AQA: Paper 2; Edexcel: Paper 1; Eduqas: Paper 2.

2 No – all exams are closed book.

3 Yes, on AQA and Edexcel, but not for Eduqas.

4 AQA: 45 minutes; Edexcel: 50 minutes; Eduqas: 45 minutes.

5 It is better to use shorter, embedded quotations than longer ones as this will enable you to analyse language in greater detail and add clarity to your answer.

6 Yes.

7 Planning ensures that you have enough to say and enables you to organise your answer so that it is easier to write and easier to follow. It also means you do not miss out any crucial areas you wish to cover.

8 Check back over your answers for errors and ensure you have included all the ideas you wished to include.

Assessment Objectives and skills (p. 71)

1 Your ability to read, understand and respond to texts. Students should be able to: maintain a critical style and develop an informed personal response; use textual references, including quotations, to support and illustrate interpretations.

2 You should be able to analyse the language, form and structure used by a writer to create meanings and effects, using relevant subject terminology where appropriate.

3   Show understanding of the relationship between texts and the contexts in which they were written.

4   The examiner should be able to understand what you are writing and accurate spelling, punctuation and grammar will enable them to do this more easily.

5   It depends which exam board you are studying. Look back to see which AOs are not covered by your board.

6   No. This will not gain many marks. You need to also explain how the device is used and the effect it may have on readers. It is much better to identify fewer devices and to explain their effect in greater detail. If you are entered for Edexcel you will not gain marks for identifying devices at all, as AO2 is not assessed on this text.

STUDY AND REVISE
for GCSE